The Coparazzi

Vincent Casale

AUTHOR'S NOTE
Enclosed find secrets about me that could only now be
revealed. I know my family understands and it is my hope you
will as well.

With love and gratitude, I dedicate this book to my family,
Christine, Jessica, Lindsey, and Emily.
You always keep me grounded.

Acknowledgements

I wish to thank the following for their generous time, support, guidance, and especially patience, in the advancement of my book. I am forever grateful.

A family of talented assistants, artists and on the spot technicians: Christine Casale, Jessica Casale, Lindsey Casale, Emily Casale, and Matthew Casale.

My 'Hooks', retired NYPD Homicide Detective, Ron Cadieux, retired NYPD, Officer Al Pizzano, and my dear uncle, Bobby Casale.

Extra pair of eyes: Anne Mutarelli, and Carlos Cunha, Ph.D.

The Long Island Writers Guild Network; Peter Garenani, Dennis Kotch, and Joe Giacalone.

Marilyn Olsen and the authors of the Public Safety Writers Association.

The New York City Police Department, and The NYPD Movie-TV Unit.

My editor, Mary Huber, who with honesty and dedication worked tirelessly to shape this novice's manuscript into a book.

Tim Dees, for mystical geek skills.

When boys grow up they want to be movie stars,
rock stars, or policemen.

The Prequel

Celebrity worship is a curse. Like the effect of a drug, it takes hold of an impressionable mind in dire need of a role model, someone starving for recognition early in life. This was certainly true in my case.

However, celebrity worship is not only my obsession. The stories of all kinds of celebrities — movie stars, politicians, athletes, even criminals and famous businessmen — are intoxicating fodder that feeds the vivid imaginations of people from all walks of life.

Yet, I did experience some fine, uplifting moments in my many encounters with celebrities. However, the ideal goal would be to separate a passing phase from an obsession. Easier said than done for those stricken with personality obsessive disorder! For some, stargazing can be simply a hobby — like golfing or woodworking — however, for the person inherently obsessed, the absorbing fascination with others' lives can create considerable stress.

My focus on the lives of "important" people began when I was a child. I have defining memories of — plainly and simply — being hooked on celebrity, and it all started with television. In the 60s and 70s, the heroes of my youth were right there on the boob tube: Batman, The Munsters, The Brady Bunch, Zorro, and endless, omnipotent cartoon characters.

How 'bout them Bradys? Wasn't everyone's life just as hunky-dory as theirs? Hell, I don't think their dog, Tiger, even took a crap. Couldn't we all be the heroes that Batman was? Even The Munsters were not as dysfunctional as their makeup would indicate. Back then, it was only the characters whom we knew and related to, it was not the stars who lived the charade.

Soon, my interest in the lives of celebrities became an insatiable fascination. Many a time I couldn't concentrate on more important subjects, such as schoolwork. That's not to say I was a stalker in the sicko sense, I simply wanted to be part of what I thought was a great life, where the mastery of a craft and public success meant everything.

Maybe the catalyst was the then-unknown concept of obsessive behavior. Did the parents of a previous generation think their child was obsessive simply because that child did something strange? For example, like a squirrel, I would hoard my candy. However, unlike the squirrel, I often would be unable to "dig up" my hidden sweet treats. Frequently, I would leave bits of candy unwrapped to savor for another day; my mother would find them stashed all over the house.

In sheer frustration, she'd yell, "Can't you just eat the goddamned candy? It's not like you're deprived!"

Why was I like that? I have no idea. I would cry if I got a speck of dirt on my hands, or on a clean white sweater. Scuffed shoes caused a fit of anxiety. For years, any clothing I purchased new would hang in the closet or remain neatly folded in the drawer, unworn for weeks. Sometimes, months would go by before I'd wear it. A nagging thought would linger in the back of my mind for days. Would people assume my behavior to be, um, a bit strange?

At any rate, I grew up interweaving my personal obsessions with my television fantasies, thinking I really could be the person right there on the screen. Television was supposed to be a tool to shut us up. For me, it was nothing short of mesmerizing. Trancelike, I'd be quiet as a mouse as I became lost in the adventures playing out on the boob tube.

Television became all too real to me one summer in the late 60s. I lived in Flushing, Queens, a few blocks from Main Street and near the local movie theater appropriately named, are you ready for this? — the Main Street Movie Theater. Unlike today's multiplex entertainment behemoths, it was simply an average neighborhood movie house that ran double features. A dim, sort of mysterious place, redolent of stale cigarette smoke, it had sloping floors, cushy seats, and heavy, dusty, floor-length curtains. Above our heads was a balcony from which, once in awhile, buttered popcorn would rain down on our heads.

That was the theater in which the talented Fran Drescher worked as a ticket girl before her very brief role in Saturday Night Fever. You might remember her starring in the popular sitcom, The Nanny.

On one memorable day, the entire population of neighborhood Batman fans crowded in front of the theater because the Caped Crusader and the Boy Wonder were scheduled to make a live appearance, one of many, I'm sure, to promote the release of the first Batman motion picture. Since it was a clear, sunny day, it seemed that throngs of people—half the town maybe—had gathered on the sidewalk in front of the celluloid palace. Eagerly, they pressed forward to catch a glimpse of the stars who would be arriving momentarily.

Finally, like all good things worth waiting for, a Greyhound bus slowly and ponderously pulled up to the curb in front of our theater. Yes, it was a bus, not the Batmobile. Even so, the hiss of airbrakes releasing pressure caused many a young heart to flutter—the heroes were about to disembark and walk among us! At first, we could not see the Dynamic Duo because dark curtains covered the rear windows of the Greyhound. We kids waited with great anticipation for our favorite characters to step out of the bus that had, in our eyes, turned into a magical chariot. Batman and Robin did not disappoint. How could they? BAM-POW! They shot off the bus flashing their brilliant smiles and donning their utility belts. They zigzagged straight into the theater without stopping as a crescendo of cheers roared from the sidewalk. For me, just seeing them— in the flesh!—was all that mattered; there was no need for pictures and autographs.

The air rang with kid-screeches, "Batman! Hey, Batman!" "Over here, Robin!" "We love you!"

I still don't remember if they even stuck around. It didn't

matter. Just a glimpse of their colorful cartoon-like images captivated us, and we spent the day bedazzled by the very sight of them, however brief it was.

Who knew at the time that our heroes would turn out to be fallible? As children, we knew nothing of Hollywood's horndogs and their revolving trailer-door exploits.

No matter, those were the days for me. The magic of movies, whether on the big silver screen in the theater or on the tiny TV screen in the living room, was even greater than the lure of a regularly scheduled television show. I will always remember us, my brothers, my sister, and I, sitting cross-legged on our living room rug, fresh from our baths (where the feeling of new pajamas and clean wet hair was especially satisfying to me, as if it were all part of the event), our mom making snacks in the kitchen.

"Any minute," she would say, as we stared, starry eyed and entranced, at the Zenith television set that was neatly framed by the polished wood cabinet. We were waiting for the start of the annual showing of The Wizard of Oz.

Of course, these magical events occurred before the birth of video and cable, which now permit us to view any movie a thousand times. At that time, though, in our pre-technological innocence, it was like watching a major movie event. The affinity for anything "movies" continued through my childhood when my dad, knowing how sad I would feel if I missed a favorite, would wake me up late at night to watch some memorable films such as Frankenstein, The Wolfman, and anything which featured Cagney or Bogart.

"Come on, Vin, it's on," he would whisper.

Around the time I was entering my teenage years, most of my friends were becoming interested in cars and fast girls. My pals, some of whom were—as we used to say—"real tough guys," unwittingly shielded me from my innocence. I was great at acting the part, convincingly, of a delinquent with an attitude. This helped conceal my shy interior and alleviate my low self-esteem problems.

I wasn't into the nitty-gritty of car mechanics, and I put girls on a pedestal in a romantic, old-movie-genre kind of way, where the music of a floating symphony played perfect backdrop to the story, or to Frank Sinatra crooning, "We are the only couple on the floor." At such a young and impressionable age, I was in love with the idea of love, the kind that could be fuzzily warm or painfully cold. So, since my interest in tuning cars was, at best, minimal, I hitched my wagon to an obsession with movies.

Thus began my steady diet of old films, particularly Warner Brothers classic gangster flicks starring Bogart, Cagney, Raft, and Robinson. To this day, I maintain a collection of books about legendary film stars—John Wayne, Marlon Brando, James Dean, Steve McQueen and Al Pacino—those guys were the coolest! I wanted to hitch my shoulders like Cagney, smoke like Bogie, brood like Brando, ride the chariot with Ben Hur, or even stroll down the Yellow Brick Road. To save my life, I couldn't quote from books, but I sure could recite lines from movies with ease! I fell in love with the seductive darkness of a movie theater; perhaps it was to escape my own insecurities that I couldn't articulate at the time? I escaped with the same fervor that I might have experienced at a baseball doubleheader or my friends might have experienced with their heads stuck under the hood of a Chevy.

As it turned out, the celluloid bug never left me. I felt like that obsessed kid from the movie, Fade to Black, only I didn't have to deal with the murders. Of course, The Godfather became my all-time favorite movie. I remember seeing not only The Godfather, but also Bonnie and Clyde, as well, at the Main Street Theater while sitting in the balcony, smoking cigarettes.

I was mesmerized by the explosion and expression of colors that elaborated the choreographed violence. Sitting high up there in a real old-style movie house, I was embraced by deep shades of looming crimson drapery, as beams of flickering light from the lens of the rolling projector lanced through the smoky haze and lit up the screen with action. The setting was simple, yet the ambience was golden. I knew I would never forget such experiences.

***

In 1978, I was nineteen years old. After high school, I was lazy and lacked ambition, which was just fine at the time, I thought. So, I quit my union job working at a film laboratory with my father. One day, in an uncharacteristic burst of energy, I decided to uproot my life and travel to California to stay with my Uncle Joe for a while.

A thousand times he had said to me in his raspy gangster voice, "What have you got going on there in New York?"

He was right, and since I also needed to escape the aura of an unrequited love, that was it—I was suddenly out of there, heading for the Golden West of my dreams. The pilgrimage had begun; the horizon of my expectations had suddenly broadened beyond my wildest dreams to Hollywood, where my uncle lived in a big furnished apartment. Though the furnishings were tacky, mostly orange and dull gold, it didn't matter; I had made it to the storied West Coast, where I was going to meet movie stars, and maybe even get discovered in a supermarket, considering how incredibly handsome I was. At last, the adventure was at hand! Uncle Joe was a jeweler by trade, who was trying to break into the movie business (again) as a half-assed agent. Frequently without an office to set up "shop," he used payphones to make his contacts, all the time pretending he was sitting at his desk. Fifty percent of his "big mogul" motive was attracting women.

Our family probably thought my uncle was a kook; I mean, really—a man his age still plugging away with the idea he would one day become a successful agent representing performing artists! I was certain that he fled to Los Angeles instead of remaining in New York for that very reason. He wanted to leave the doubting Thomases behind.

At any rate, California certainly was disappointing. Mostly, in the first few months, I was acutely lonely. In Los Angeles, especially, we were surrounded by many "wannabes," all sure they were on the verge of becoming legitimate actors, writers, producers, or IMPORTANT PEOPLE.

In our apartment complex, hoards of well-oiled men and women sat by the pool, clutching bulky landline phones (no cell phones back then!). Their telephone cords stretched for yards along the pool deck and snaked through shrubbery all the way back through their apartment doors as they sunbathed and waited in vain for the phone to ring with THE CALL. In retrospect—and isn't hindsight always productive?—I should have invested in telephone cords.

The endless, pointless chatter and manufactured excitement about the movie business began having a dulling effect on me. Soon, I desperately missed New York and the comfort of my friends. Yet, I stuck it out a little while longer, though I realized I would also have to get, of all things, a (gasp!) JOB. My end of the bargain with Uncle Joe was to contribute to the apartment rent once I got on my feet. Also, if I were to have any staying power in L.A., it was a must that I enroll in some kind of acting classes. My uncle encouraged me to network, read plays, and practice lines with other actors. I wasn't opposed to the idea; it had been something I always dreamed of, yet I had never been this far from home, and I was feeling truly out of my element—not the best scenario for tip-top performance or even productivity.

I must admit, though, that it was thrilling to see actors just walking around on their everyday errands. Many character actors I had seen for years on television would pop up in supermarkets, on the streets, in bars, and in Schwab's, the famous drug store/diner where legend has it that gorgeous sweater girl, Lana Turner, was discovered at the counter drinking a soda. She must have looked ravishing.

We did experience some very exciting bright spots; of particular note was when Uncle Joe somehow scored tickets to the stunning premiere of Grease, which was showing at Grauman's Chinese Theater. Grauman's is where legends of Hollywood still haunt the sidewalks of Hollywood Boulevard; it's where the handprints and footprints of icons are embedded forever in the sidewalk that paves the way into that great theater.

I landed on the sidelines of the red carpet prior to the screening of Grease. It seemed like a million miles from home. Hundreds of fans went wild when John Travolta and Olivia Newton John's car pulled to the curb. People were screaming for autographs, a handshake, a touch, or just a wave. I knew then that it was all about the movie stars; it was not about the producers, the directors, or the executives. The heavenly adoration was reserved exclusively for those on the big screen.

Dressed in slick leather, Travolta and Olivia (hot, hot, hot!) were decked out like their characters, Danny and Sandy. Travolta, his magnificent hair greased back, exuded cool. Olivia's bright golden hair was accentuated by her black leather jacket and black stretch pants. At the curb, the adored ones exited from their hot, greased-lightning car, which was also featured in the film. The crowd's obsession was at a contagious fever pitch, and the excitement of this major movie premiere thrilled me beyond words. When the celebrities appeared, I envisioned, almost in slow motion, the day that it would be me, beaming and waving to my adoring fans.

Like many in love with the film business, I was blown away. After the experience with Grease, I was feeling hopped up. I wanted to meet a celebrity first hand, not from a distance.

Uncle Joe knew many people from the early New York theater scene, but his lofty stage visions faded fast when he realized that loyalty to the East Harlem neighborhood would decide his fate, even though Burt Lancaster and Anthony Franciosa were from the same neighborhood.

Although he was only a half-assed agent, my uncle did have a few important connections and, one day, he took me to visit with actor Tony Mordente, famous for playing the character of Action in West Side Story. My uncle knew Mordente from the acting classes of his youth, where his unrealized dreams had died on the vine of wishful thinking.

I was delighted to go and meet Action. I loved West Side Story and the characters of the film gang. The Jets, with their leather wristbands and thick black garrison belts buckled off to the side of their jeans, were the street guys of old.

Tony Mordente was perched on a wall in his garden with his feet dangling. As he casually chatted with my uncle, he pulled a switchblade from his pocket, flicked it open with a practiced snap of his wrist, à la Action, and began to groom his fingernails. My uncle laughed.

"Look at you," he said. "Still Action."

Looking back now—and isn't hindsight wonderful?—I don't know why I was so impressed. Tony was still playing with knives fifteen years after West Side Story.

My stay in Los Angeles was brief. My uncle persistently encouraged me to start acting, and he did everything he could to help me. He almost succeeded. In the end, though, missing my home and my friends won out. I often wondered what would have happened if I had just given my acting dream a little more time and effort. I imagine that my uncle harbored the same thoughts when he was young.

However, giving it time and more effort did not seem to be my thing. Perhaps I suffered from Attention Deficit Disorder. I'll never know. Before going West to pursue my dream of performing on the silver screen, I had attempted acting on my home turf. Secretly. No one in the neighborhood knew that, although my friends were aware of my love affair with movies.

For a very brief period after I finished high school, I snuck off to Manhattan and attended an acting school on Bank Street in Greenwich Village, where the likes of Steve McQueen and Robert De Niro had studied their craft at HB Studios. There, I was encouraged by the positive feedback from the instructors when I acted out a monologue from The Detective Story.

"I wish I could take my brain out..."

Strolling on the cobblestone streets and the tree-lined sidewalks of the Village, I was taken to an airy place in my head. It was euphoria with a touch of Bohemia. Yet, I harbored a secret fear of ending up in the gritty reality of my blue-collared neighborhood. Jobs were where it was "at," especially union jobs, and those were best landed immediately after high school. Forget college. So, if I were seen wandering the streets of Greenwich Village or schmoozing at an outdoor café with struggling actors, I would have been laughed at. In my neighborhood, I knew respected guys who wanted to be musicians; hell, who wouldn't want to be a rock star or a singer performing with girls screaming and panting at your feet?

On the other hand, acting was not a respectable aspiration. Although, when I was planning to leave for L.A., some of the girls we hung around with confidently remarked, "Try to be an actor while you're out there."

Yet, it was one thing to be told, "you should be an actor," or "you look like so and so.... " and it was quite another to actually attend an acting school!

***

I left for California with the sound of "Layla" still in my ears. I returned to "Disco Duck."

Scene I

In 1986, I was a young cop with the New York City Police Department. It was the time when the new breed of police officer came in all shapes, sizes, and colors. After only two years on the job, I was already feeling the boredom that many patrol officers experience when spending too much time sitting in cars and standing around on foot posts and parades, not to mention the dawning realization that I wasn't going to change the world. My career as a cop was not what I assumed it would be. Although I was diligent in my duties, I was no shining star.

I often daydreamed. Unfortunately, my exploratory thoughts were not usually about the possibilities of enhancing my career as a police officer who was scoring numerous big arrests, excelling on a plain-clothes assignment, or studying hard for a coveted promotion. Other than counting the time it would take to walk a block, I would indulge my senses with thoughts of an impressionable nightlife or relish the ideas of my childhood addiction and mentally wander in the make-believe world of movies.

I imagined playing an important part in some notable universe. Yet, I was attracted to the police force because we officers exist in the spotlight; people are aware of us, for better or worse. The partying was plentiful and constant; it went on for many days and nights. I had a friend who used to call himself, "The Blue Magnet."

"This is how we attract chicks. Like the stars do," he said, frequently.

"Blue Magnet" wasn't the only one in our bunch with a semi-glamorous or just plain strange nickname. We had "Casino," "Lance

Romance," "Smurf," "Shark," "Monty," "JJ," and "Meat." We even had our very own "Monster."

We all drank and partied as if our lives depended on it, and I was pursuing a lifestyle more akin to the wild style of Frank Sinatra than it was to the quiet, dignified style of Jimmy Stewart.

Certainly, we weren't rock stars, but we cops did OK because of our uniform. It helped that nurses and late-tour emergency workers were on similar schedules, thus allowing us to roam at night, seven days a week, while the 9-to-5 world slept in their beds.

We weren't intimidating in a menacing sort of way, and we mingled with most people; but our group was a pack of cocky bastards. With attitude. Piss off if you don't like us!

Our bartender buddy told us that other local precincts' cops were commenting about us.

"Who do those 1-0-9 assholes think they are?" they asked.

I numbered my share of episodes in which I dove deep into the pit of classic alcoholic binges. Hey, why not? Hadn't many cool celebrities done the same? Strangely, I actually derived a modicum of pleasure when some questioned my unkempt and gaunt appearance after one binge. I thought it was cool to get the attention, however critical. Ironically, my repulsive behavior destroyed my relationship with the woman who encouraged me to take the police exam in the first place. She was the person I promised to walk the straight and narrow for.

My immaturity was probably a case of arrested development. I had a hard time trying to grow up. "Fairy tales can come true; they can happen to you..." blah, blah, blah! Perhaps because I didn't possess the chops in my own life, and I wasn't exactly a go-getter, I still marveled at the way others were living their lives, especially celebrities who seemed to have it all. However, out in the real world, I was a police office, and that is what I should have been concentrating on. Being a cop certainly wasn't anything to complain about. As a matter of fact, I relished those moments when I felt quite proud. It was an honor to be one of New York's Finest.

I had been fortunate up to that point in my career. I knew the right people, and they assigned me to a relatively quiet precinct in the northern section of Queens. Who knows, maybe if I had been assigned to a high-crime area, I might have been more ambitious and less dreamy.

Still, with calm comes boredom. In the universe of policing where a cop isn't designed or entrusted to save the world, monotony is inevitable. I began to wonder what could be more fulfilling than patrolling the same city streets day after day. Did there exist a better niche for me?

***

I began this chronicle in 1986, instead of in my rookie year of 1984, because that was about the time that fate stepped in. I had learned through the police grapevine some wonderful news about a special detail I was previously not aware of. I don't even remember exactly where it was that I heard of this incontrovertible news, but I do remember immediately calling around to "my" people who had helped me get assigned to a Queen's stationhouse. I was determined to ingratiate myself and get assigned to this special uniformed Unit within the NYPD.

Appropriately entitled, "The New York City Police Department's Movie and Television Unit" (informally known as the "Movie Unit"), this elite team was created to assist the motion picture and television industries whenever they were in New York City to film a production on our "set" — the great streets and skyline of New York. Police officers assigned to the Movie Unit had one job — to protect, serve and safeguard movie sets and personnel from nefarious characters, as well as to facilitate and control the busy and complicated traffic conditions often caused by the presence of the production crews.

Could I have possibly imagined being assigned to the Movie Unit? Could I believe that such a Unit designed for me existed within the confines of my chosen profession? I was joyously stunned by the concept and instantly envious of any police officer fortunate enough to be assigned to such a dream detail. I wanted with all my fiber to be a part of that elite Movie Unit; it was the niche I had been searching for. Being a cop to the stars became a position I yearned for as earnestly as anything or any job I had ever lusted after.

Many police officers with my minimal time on the job (not quite three years), would rather have worked toward the coveted gold shield of detective, but not me. I wanted to be around the movies, and I thought about it nervously and consciously for some time. After forwarding my application to the Movie Unit, my next step was to get on the phone and call as many friends and peers I could think of in the hope of securing what is called a "Hook."

"Hook" is police lingo; it isn't the opening paragraph of a book that piques the reader's interest. A "Hook," or a "Rabbi" as they are sometimes called, is someone with great connections who could receive and return a favor based on their reputation or the number of friends they have. A "Hook" is usually a high-ranking person in the police department who is able to cut through the formalities and speed the process of a direct transfer from a precinct to a specialized detail like the Movie Unit.

My quest was not going to be easy, because the Movie Unit consisted of only eighteen cops in a department of 36,000. Nothing is inevitable in the bureaucracy of the NYPD. Others with a bigger "Hook" could easily sideswipe those of us with a lesser "Hook."

The first order of business for me was to get on the horn and call another one of my uncles, Uncle Bob. He worked at a Catholic church in Astoria, Queens. His office mate was a very nice woman whose husband was a sergeant assigned to Police Headquarters. See how it works?

"Hey, Unc, I know your friend already helped me in Queens, but boy, do I want this gig!"

Of course my uncle replied, "Hey, I'll do my best!"

I knew this was a big favor to ask of Uncle Bob, because it

would be my second time around for such a request. However, he was a great guy and really wanted to help me. Like most of my uncles, he was old-school; family came first. In addition to asking Uncle Bob to help me, I also reached out to a long-ago family friend who had twenty years on the job and who was in good standing as a long-time delegate in the police union. He knew the union president, Phil Caruso, quite well. I had not seen this old family friend in years, but even so, isn't that what old friends are for?

After the formalities of reintroducing myself via the phone call were over, I said, "Al, how the hell are you? How's the family? Yeah, I'm good. Job's fine. I remember when you first told me….No, not married yet….By the way, there's this Movie Unit that I heard about…."

Al was realistic and told me that, more than likely, I would have to wait because I was still fairly new on the job, and there were guys with a "Hook" who had been around awhile. So, I remained stuck in my patrol duties and nightlife adventures with my buddies. However, after wandering the bar scene ad nauseam, I decided to back off from the endless partying. Sometime later, I met a new girl, Christine, with whom I was destined to be in a serious relationship. The attraction was instant; I was a sucker for slender blondes with delicate complexions. After a time, I even enlisted Christine in my quest for a transfer. Her father was a retired NYPD Homicide Detective. He had to know someone!

"C'mon," I asked, as if I'd known her for years, and it was my right. "Please, it's me after all. Your dad could help me out in a big way…. He'll listen to you."

Now I had all my feelers out there, and it was just a matter of waiting. As police officers like to say, it became "hurry up and wait." That wait could be a long and anxious process, especially if any one of the aforementioned people had to connect my name to third and fourth parties.

It took more than two years before I could get squeezed into a spot on the coveted detail. In the interim, I went about my business, my police duties, and my deepening relationship with Christine. During much of that time, I would dream of the Movie Unit. Whenever I picked up a newspaper — and I did that with regularity — I would see photographs taken by the paparazzi of celebrities filming on New York sets.

Not knowing when my big, longed-for assignment would happen, I nevertheless hoped beyond hope. But still, I had to suppress those wishful aspirations in case my dream job went up in smoke. I also had to be on my best behavior because any complaints against me, civilian or departmental, no matter how minor, could jeopardize my desired transfer.

Scene II

By 1989, recruitment in the police department was at an all-time high. Press coverage was extremely affable toward the NYPD. Besides combating crime, cops were rescuing bridge jumpers and helping injured stray dogs. The detectives were also in the news with their famous "perp walks," escorting high-profile suspects out of the stationhouse directly into the lights of the press. Many of these detectives were impeccably dressed, all duded up for their close-ups.

Mayor Ed Koch, frequently in the spotlight himself, promoted the idea that the NYPD was recognized as the best in the world. It was the end of an era for the colorful mayor, who was completing his third term.

The Patrolman's Benevolent Association was particularly grateful to Koch and bade him farewell with a grand dinner in his honor. After all, it was Koch who had been responsible for beefing up manpower in the NYPD while also securing for the police one of their best monetary contracts in the long history of the Department.

Those were the days! It was a heady time when cops were on the move. There were retirements, promotions, and changing of assignments. There was also room in many of the department's fine details. It was my time at last! I was still patrolling the streets of Flushing, New York, when my transfer came down. By this time, I had been assigned to the precinct's fairly new CPOP Unit, the Community Patrol Officers Program.

The NYPD was eager to enhance its relationship with the community, so the powers that be devised a plan that would enable the cops to get back on close terms with the civilian populace by implementing the new CPOP program. With CPOP, police officers would once again hit the streets and ingratiate themselves with the civilian population. We began by walking the same, steady beat every day.

We stopped in to say, "Hi, how're ya' doin'?" to shopkeepers.

We watched bus and taxi stops, and generally were nice guys to the average citizen. We maintained the appearance of the old beat cop our parents remembered, without the whacking sound of threatening nightsticks.

However, after a time, this assignment became like many I would take on, boring. There were days where I just didn't want to placate the citizenry of Flushing, Queens. But CPOP had the advantage of allowing specific days off and flexible scheduled hours. This suited us much better than the rotating shifts required on patrol.

One quiet afternoon, after a long and uneventful tour, I strolled into the stationhouse and passed the lieutenant on the front desk.

"Hey, Vincenzo," he called out. "How's the goom?"

Obviously the lieutenant was Italian. He was a heck of a guy who always asked the male cops about a "goom," which meant he was inquiring about the guy's mistress, otherwise known as a second girlfriend. There was plenty of gossip that circulated in New York precincts, but this lieutenant asked just for the sheer fun of it.

After responding, "Very good, Lou," I continued walking by Carmine, the cop who was manning the switchboard where all the calls came into the precinct except 911 calls.

"Hey, Casale, congrats on your transfer."

"Transfer?" I whipped around. "What transfer? Really? Or are you breaking 'em on me?"

"I wouldn't joke," he said, earnestly.

Normally, I would not have questioned his comment, but Carmine was a prankster who was always ribbing people and goofing around to make people laugh. Still, it didn't click in that instant for me because I had tried to put the hope of joining the Movie Unit on my mind's backburner, especially after CPOP.

Wait a minute, I thought. Maybe CPOP is cutting its manpower, and I've been kicked back to patrol? Shit!

"Yeah, you're transferred," Carmine continued. "Movie Unit. Who the hell do you know?"

"What? Are you kidding?" I hissed.

I realized I had lowered my voice, perhaps because I was in disbelief. Maybe I was afraid the secret would get out, and someone else would steal my spot with a quick phone call after they heard about this wonderful detail.

"It just came down, Vince. Check the log, you lucky bastard. Finally, someone's gettin' outta' here."

I shook my fellow officer's hand as if he had been responsible for this glorious turn of events, and I walked away, shaken, but I felt a wide grin spread across my face. Quickly, but inconspicuously, I made a beeline to the logbook, which was behind the big desk in the top right drawer. Most cops checked the log see if they had a day off. I was seeking much more!

There it was, "Report to the Movie TV Unit, 0700 hrs. Monday." I checked again and even read it a third time. I was completely floored. I couldn't calm down the rest of the day. I called my girlfriend with the excitement of a lottery winner ringing in my voice. I was like a rookie after his first arrest. I checked the log again on my way out. Now it was certain that I was leaving patrol duties. Excluding serious, victim-type crimes such as robbery and burglary, I was rid of the complaining civilian population with their constant griping about rabbles and loiterers, the annoying noise, and the irritable street peddlers.

Their incessant questions of "Where is this?" and "What if that...?"

The insignificant squabbles between merchants and customers, and the forever-unruly parking conditions were about to become mere irritations of the past.

All I kept thinking was that the grass must be greener on the other side of patrol. The fantasy to escape was building, even though my getaway was less than a week away. Let someone else take my post and deal with that disorderly drunk who shit himself. I was no longer going to patrol down Main Street and risk walking into a melting pot of trouble. I no longer wanted to sit on my ass in night lockup.

My new assignment was all I could think about; it even took precedence over my personal life. Any talk of seriously furthering my romantic relationship was put on the back burner. What the hell, I had failed at love in the past. All that mattered now was that I was going to Hollywood. Hollywood on the Hudson!

Scene III

Predictably, after the high wore off, nervousness set in. My first days in the Movie Unit were anxious ones. Lieutenant Gasper, the Movie Unit's commanding officer, initiated me by taking me out for the day to introduce me to my Movie Unit comrades. The lieutenant, of course, had to bore me with the rules and regulations bullshit. There was actually a rules pamphlet. It was a stapled, two-page outline consisting of the usual police rhetoric about maintaining professionalism, especially around those in the film industry.

The most laughable rule, even to a newcomer like myself, was the one that stated, "Under no circumstances should a police officer accost or annoy any persons involved in the production, either for photographs or autographs." Even old thin-lipped and red-faced Lt. Gasper, who previously had been assigned to Internal Affairs, was not going to enforce that one.

So the conversation was, "No, boss, I certainly will not bother anyone. Absolutely, I will do as I am asked and act professionally at all times. Yes, sir!"

Of course, this was all a mere formality in case they looked for an excuse to boot your ass out of the Movie Unit. That way, "The Job" can say, "I told you so."

After I met the paper pushers in the office, the lieutenant took me out into the field to get acquainted with the cops. All the while I was wondering what movie set I would see first.

"Hey, how are ya'? Nice t'meet cha!" Now, where the hell are the movie stars?

There were no stars during the first days; the only shoots

were commercials for television. Where was Pacino?

I became familiar with the goings-on in the Movie Unit as well as with the police officers, most of whom had the same time on the job as I did. However, my first exposure to the movie scene was disappointing to say the least. I got my feet wet with a few commercial spots for television, both domestic and foreign. I figured since I was new, I wasn't going to get a chance to work at the choice movie scenes filming around town.

The first commercial spot was a doozy. I had to stand on the pedestrian ramp that stretched down on the Brooklyn side of its namesake bridge. A crew of Japanese directors was hunkered over their stars; small toy action figures the size of the "Rock'em, Sock'em Robots." They were trying to get the little robots to move in unison so that when production was complete, it would appear that the robots were as large as life and walking the length of the bridge. All for the sake of selling batteries!

It was a windy day, and I had to grab hold of my hat a few times, wondering the whole time, is this what I'm in for? Should I have stayed in the security of a warm radio car? Even on a foot post, I could have ducked inside somewhere to get out of the elements.

Nevertheless, I approached each assignment with enthusiasm. I was getting close to my first night shift, and I thought, this is it! Since I was new, I dared not ask the old timer, wiry-haired Officer Spinell, who was in charge of roll call, what the assignment entailed. Many times I would hope that Officer Gurney would answer the phone. As Spinell's fill-in, she was a world of difference in the personality department.

***

When I arrived in Brooklyn, it just had the feel of a real movie. I was finally going to see some celebrities. There was a bright mist fogging the entire block. The brilliant beams of light from the production company lamps illuminated the mist, causing it to glow.

The assignment required three men—two burly, olive-skinned veteran police officers and me. To my compatriots, my being new in the Movie Unit made me a rookie again, and they treated me as such, casually walking away every chance they got. It would start with a question from me.

"Hey, guys...."

And, when I received grunted, one-word replies, I felt like I had been whistling in the wind. Still, they were mostly cordial, and that's all I could have asked for.

We were in Bay Ridge, Brooklyn, on the set of a made-for-TV movie. The story line was about police detectives. Richard Crenna and Cliff Gorman were the stars, and I concentrated on trying to spot them. Because it was a cool, misty night, threatening heavy rain, the streets were empty, and I didn't get to see the actors because production had moved inside a house to film interior scenes.

Then, like a shot, my tour that night was over. However, I did procure my first taste of a motion picture street set with lighting, sights of cameras, sound wires, gaffers and electricians, all milling about in the small doorway of the house. I also became aware that movie production spared no cost. Most people would never allow the mess of a film crew to disrupt their homes, unless they were paid big bucks, as the owner of the Brooklyn home was. On the other hand, some folks though it was a big deal if they saw their living room played out in a movie scene.

That night, I also received my first introduction to the craft services table, which is a smorgasbord of snacks for all the crew members to indulge in between meals. There was no shortage of hot and cold drinks, cakes and fruit, and plenty of candy for the picking. The craft service table was set up under a tarp because of the foul weather, and I stood there munching on goodies with cold rainwater dripping down the back of my neck. This was great for me, though, because my own refrigerator was bare most of the time.

***

Eventually, I got a call for the real deal. Telly Savalas was in town to shoot, The Return of Kojak. The lollipop-sucking police hero was filming with Kevin Dobson, who played Kojak's old sidekick and faithful detective, Crocker.

Kojak always addressed Crocker at the top of his inimitable voice, "Crocker!"

I responded to the set from my home, another reason why I knew this detail was for me. No uniformed roll calls, no standing at attention, no speeches about making arrests and writing summonses. All I had to do was pack my uniform in the trunk of my car and go. Certainly, this assignment was right up my alley, and the location that surrounds the charming Gramercy Park made the trip even more worthwhile.

On the verge of meeting Telly Savalas, I reflected on some personal family history. Another uncle, gray-haired and sophisticated, was a restaurateur in the 70s and early 80s. His restaurant, Tre Amici, was an elegant Italian eatery, complete with black-and-white leather seating and stylish décor.

Mr. Savalas and his crew would frequent the restaurant when they were in town shooting the original Kojak series. There, in the entrance lobby to the restaurant, mounted on my uncle's wall of fame that featured celebrities and athletes, was a group shot of the star and his crew with my uncle and his staff. That proudly displayed photo was one of the first he ever received.

I thought, now it's going to be my turn to put a photo up on that wall!

So began my history of failed photography. I didn't have a camera on set that day, and I was assigned to work alone.

Frantically, I wondered, how can I get my hands on a camera? Maybe another Movie Unit cop will show?

I had a great fear of "getting my feet wet," so to speak, because I would have to be the one to ask Savalas for permission to take his photo. I procrastinated with what would become a habit of mine — to always think there will be a tomorrow. "Tomorrow" meant that I'd better purchase the required equipment, and fast. A trusty camera, preferably one I could fit comfortably in the back pocket of my uniform pants.

The other officers in the Movie Unit had already amassed quite a collection of photos for their private galleries and, if I wanted to keep some sort of pace, I would have to get started.

One senior officer, PO Capezzio (one of the olive-skinned guys), possessed probably the best collection of anyone, cop or otherwise. He had his picture taken with legends, including Frank Sinatra, Marlon Brando, and James Cagney. Capezzio had a natural flair for inserting himself into the movie zone. His technique was nothing short of aggressive.

Of course, the uniform helped. Capezzio also had the knack for telling the stories behind his picture conquests. In his woven tales, it was as if the celebrity became his pal. And I thought I had an obsession!

"Sinatra invited me into his trailer," he would say, and, "Brando went out of his way to say hello to me."

I, on the other hand, was still too nervous to approach any celebrity. This shy behavior would get me nowhere if I didn't change my hold-back fear into a ballsy approach. Still, for the time being, I could rely on my fellow officers to break the ice for me, if and when they were around. Snapping photographs would be no easy task, but the result would be much better than simply pasting movie memorabilia and magazine photos into a notebook like I did when I was a kid.

Word had it that Telly Savalas loved New York cops. He even owned an honorary police shield given to him by the Police Commissioner years before, when he played the famous TV detective. I would later witness him pose for pictures with many of the precinct cops who asked him. Yet, here I was; assigned to his shoot without another Movie Unit cop who could snap a photo of us. So, I hoped that I would soon get another chance at a picture with Savalas.

***

One morning soon after, Kevin Dobson was on the set standing by the old brownstone St. George Church in Gramercy Park; it was the perfect location to ask for a photo. Dobson was also known to be friendly to the police.

I worked with my friend, Officer Tom Love, on the set.

"Tom, I see Dobson. I want to get a picture."

"Sure, I'll be around," he said. "Just let me know when you're ready and I'll take it."

Tom was a great guy, and one of my "Blue Magnet" buddies, but he wasn't into pictures. He was biding his time until he was called into the NYC Fire Department. Not only Tom, but also many other cops were making the switch to what they deemed a better job. In the interim, Tom would do his own thing, disappearing most of the day, trying to meet women.

So, without Tom's help, I would be unable to approach Dobson. I realized I didn't have a camera that day anyway, so it was futile all around.

Obviously, if I didn't break the ice with the actors, I couldn't start my own album. It shouldn't have been such a big deal. After all, I was a cop, and most people respected that. Hell, even the non-Movie Unit cops were getting in on the action.

Besides the local precincts' Movie Units, Highway Units enjoyed the temporary glamour associated with movie-making, and I saw a photo of a bunch of them in the newspaper, huddled in a group shot with The Rolling Stones. The cops were all on their motorcycles and the Stones were standing with them, everyone smiling broadly. They were promoting the Steel Wheel Tour.

Many city cops were posing for photos with stars, especially in Manhattan, where stargazing is an everyday event. Patrolmen knew where to lurk. The best places were hotels, Broadway theaters, and television studios.

***

I had the perfect opportunity to get my photo while standing on the corner of Carmine and Bedford streets in the West Village obsessing over my failure, hoping a brother officer would be assigned with me on yet another day of shooting with Savalas.

No such luck. The Kojak crew was returning from lunch when I saw Savalas emerge from the side door of a restaurant. Up close, he was bigger than life and as bald and beautiful as he was on TV. I remember getting the same kick of excitement as when I'd seen John Travolta in the flesh more than a decade before.

Anyway, it was apparent that Savalas had tipped back a few drinks over lunch. His tie was askew, he walked a bit slanted, and he was wearing a super glow on his face.

His crooked smile complimented his thoughts, whatever they were. Not having my camera in my back pocket was the perfect excuse to blow another easy opportunity.

Next time, I thought for the thousandth time.

It was like when you see a pretty girl and you're dying to approach her, and it's always, I'll see her again. . . next time.

Even though there was no chance, I still paced up and down the block as if a camera would appear by magic.

***

I did see Mr. Savalas again later in the week. Kojak moved their shoot to Central Park, in front of the Bethesda Fountain, the Angel of the Waters. Onlookers formed around the top of the great stairs, but they were unable to get a good look at the famous actor. The central perimeter of the set and around the actors was obstructed by the few standing black shades, or flags, as they are called. The flags block out the unwanted light that can ruin the quality of the desired effect.

I moved to position myself when I heard the command, "Check the Gate!"

Usually, it was the cameraman who would announce he was "Checking the Gate," a phrase that meant he wanted the film to be cleared of any debris or "hair," as it's called. Only then would the director wrap up the shooting day. After the dialogue scene wrapped, Savalas gave me the perfect (and last) opportunity to get a photo — of course not deliberately.

I finally had a camera in my possession when the actor walked right by me and smiled. I frantically hoped for someone to assist me.

I had the shot, come on!

There was nobody around.

Actually, thinking there was no one around was ridiculous, because there was always someone around in eyeshot — a member of the crew, or a person passing by. After all, this was New York. Easy, right? Wrong.

Next time.... I ran with that thought for days.

Regrettably, there would be no next time. The production of Kojak ended. I never saw Telly Savalas again. The actor died in January of 1994.

Scene IV

I continued to approach each assignment with optimism and confidence, as though I would sooner or later infiltrate the world of celebrity. I felt the way a restaurant owner, a chauffeur, or a doorman at a famous nightclub might feel when they greet someone famous.

I had been in the Movie Unit only two weeks when my union "Hook" called to ask me if I thought I had made the right decision.

"Do you think it was a wise move?" he queried.

I told him I was fine. I certainly did not want to seem ungrateful, even as I paradoxically encountered some boredom. Something I always repeat in my life is second-guessing major decisions, both professionally and romantically. It is probably the result of my previously mentioned Attention Deficit Disorder.

My "Hook" still believed I would have been better served had I opted to join a more formidable detail, one that would have perhaps earned me a detective's gold shield. For a moment, I thought about those well-dressed detectives doing their perp walk. Did I really want to play cops and robbers?

Anyhow, as I weaved through a combination of excitement and monotony, I would learn how much the privileged are truly catered to. The arm of entitlement did not reach out to the folks who worked tirelessly behind the scenes of production; it was reserved for the big boys, those with status—the stars, the directors, the cameramen, the editors, and the producers.

They were the players out in the forefront; the remaining members of the human food chain took their places in the rear. Get the picture? Sure, to give some recognition to those hard-working crewmembers, production would roll their names during the movie credits, which nobody, and I mean nobody, stayed to watch in a theater.

There were the production assistants, or PAs, as they were called, who were rewarded with what appeared to be a meaningful title simply to satisfy them and make their position appear more glorified than it was. The PAs were nothing more than gofers for the lot. They constantly were sent off to "Do this," and "Do that," and "Get this," and "Get that." They were assigned to many thankless chores—the jobs that were mostly a hassle to anyone else. The PAs tried keeping outsiders away from the privileged ones by assiduously maintaining their assigned perimeters, all the while hoping they wouldn't be jostled or even roughly pushed aside.

Yes, these PAs truly are hard-working souls. They must remain out on the streets even after everyone has left the set for the day in order to keep watch and guard parking spots for the crew. They sweat in the summer and freeze in the winter. They act as unqualified bodyguards, as parking attendants, and also as traffic cops (when they thought they could get away with it). Frequently, our job was to insure that the PAs kept their activities within the bounds of realism.

Wearing their ever-present headsets, PAs dashed to and fro all over the place. Via their headsets, they were constantly receiving terse orders from the circle of production chiefs who were sitting somewhere close to the cameras.

Often, the PAs would relay the annoying commands of directors as they shouted "Quiet! Rolling!" They ducked in and around people for long and exhausting hours for crap pay.

Sometimes, they earned only eighty bucks for a sixteen-hour day.

In the PAs' minds, there was the unspoken promise that they, too, might one day move up the movie-making chain toward glory. Perhaps they would become directors commanding their very own feature films. Perhaps they would beat the odds of one in every 10,000 PAs actually achieving that rank.

I'm sure that many pedestrians on the streets of New York

have encountered annoying PAs who were dressed in grunge, frantically dashing about the set, like gnats hovering at eyes' length, then back-peddling before they can be swatted. Often, we had to intervene when a few tense encounters between PAs and the civilian populace threatened to blow up.

I always wondered if the PAs were aware of the vultures who ran Hollywood.

"My parents are still mad at me," one PA told me, after he quit law school for his celluloid dream.

He seemed like a nice Jewish kid from the suburbs, eager to break out in the world. I got the impression that even his tattoo was a rebellion from his pre-planned way of life. Inked on his body was the Grim Reaper holding a pencil, signifying the suffering for art.

Still, a lot of interesting buzz came from the mouths of babes. PAs were always filling us in on the expectations and moods of the day. Which director was demanding? Which actor was in a pissy mood? Could it be Scorsese? Or William Hurt?

Even cops got in on the rumors. They spread the word about those celebrities who were cool and those who were good about having their pictures taken. For instance, one of our veteran police officers told me that Charles Bronson and Sean Connery were not necessarily high on the idea of having their pictures taken with policemen. Another officer told me that, when a group of movie cops asked the actor, James Belushi, for a picture, they were turned down.

"Who am I, fuckin' Santa Claus?" snapped Belushi.

Meg Ryan turned down our master coparazzi, Officer Capezzio, twice. Capezzio, still sour over the first snub, became increasingly infuriated each time he told the story, especially since she'd turned him down on two separate occasions.

"The second time," he grumbled, "she had the balls to pose for a photo a minute later with a hotdog vendor."

Talk about rubbing salt in his wound!

Meg Ryan is a girl I would have dreamed of in high school, I thought.

The weather was getting chilly, but the feature films were starting to roll in. Awakenings and Ghost were filming simultaneously in the Big Apple. I was extremely pumped to be working these two films, which I knew would be crawling with movie stars. The shooting locations alone were enough to get me jacked up. Yet, right out of the gate, I blew the whole picture-taking thing with Patrick Swayze. I was right up his ass escorting him to his camper, ripe for a photo op, but I was too nervous to ask and decided to wait.

Anyway, all movie shoots took full advantage of New York's entire landscape. Scenes were shot under the lights of Times Square, and directors took full advantage of the "Old World" ambience that drenched the narrow cobblestone streets of Greenwich Village. Many scenes were set in front of the priceless brownstones in Brooklyn and in the old Bronx neighborhoods. The grand architecture of Wall Street appeared in many a movie.

***

One afternoon, while I was in the Village enjoying a lunch of good, old-fashioned pizza, I ran into my former high school teacher, Ms. Horn. Her hair was now gray, and she was a bit older, but she still wore her signature warm smile. She said she was proud of me for being a police officer. Because she was a wonderful teacher, I complimented her in return, saying that her earthy guidance was something I always remembered. Ironically, she was always encouraging me to seek solace in the arts. At the time, she thought I had a certain talent for acting, especially after I acted out the T-shirt-tearing scene from A Streetcar named Desire in class.

There I was—this puny little guy acting like the macho Brando.

"You could be so good," she had told me.

Now she was curious, even as I stood there in uniform, and she asked if I'd ever ventured into the acting business.

Because I was a little disappointed that I really hadn't done so in the conventional sense, I replied, "No, but in a way, I am."

"Wonderful," she replied. "You see, I always knew you wanted to be around movies."

When I was in high school, my teachers instinctively knew where my true interest lay because it was obvious that the only subjects I paid attention to were classes involving the arts. I really did want to be an actor. So much so that I used to secretly send out black and white 8 x 10 photos of myself to major studios, like Francis Ford Coppola's Zoetrope, with the hope of being discovered. Of course I wasn't. Never even received a response. Nada. I was naïve, I guess.

After Mrs. Horn and I enjoyed a very pleasant chat, we said our good-byes, genuinely happy to have seen each other. My high school teacher played a significant part in my educational history, and I believe she knows that.

***

A couple of days after my high school reunion of sorts, I was once again educated about the degree of separation a movie production allows those close to the privileged. For example, Robin Williams and his wife were walking on the set of Awakenings, and Robin veered off for a moment.

Members of the technical crew treated Mrs. Williams as if she, herself, were in the movie. The overextension of politeness was extraordinarily transparent. I mean, she hadn't even glanced their way before all the niceties began.

"Oh, how are you today?" and, "You look great Mrs. Williams; can I get you anything? Coffee? Juice?"

Even some of the cops in my Movie Unit fell over themselves to be nice, although they would never admit it.

"Screw them celebrities," they would mutter, but they would act in a fawning manner, regardless.

Certainly, there were some folks who were sincere, but even a layman could easily pick up the ass-kissing attitude.

If truth be told, cops loved the allure of the stars and, if anyone would listen, the officers would be glad to share their own tidbits of gossip. One lieutenant told me that, when he was a young cop assigned to a movie set in New York, Jane Fonda, the star of the film, walked by him and a bunch of officers. They were huddled in a group just chewing the fat, laughing and taking notice of the production crew, the members of which were already clamoring to kiss Ms. Fonda's ass.

As the actress passed the officers, she snidely remarked, "Is this a group of cackling geese or a pen of pigs?"

"Our smiles disintegrated on the spot," the Lou told me. "But we knew if one of us said anything…well you know, the cop always comes out the loser."

I could still see the embarrassment on his face. He wished that someone could tell the "broad" off. However, he was correct in his assumption that the cop would be the loser, and maybe even be banished off to a local precinct definitely not close to his home.

Another veteran policeman told me of a conversation he just "happened" to hear. Perhaps it's not eavesdropping if it's sort of accidental? He was assigned to a commercial shoot in which the actress was the gorgeous wife of a famous hockey player. During the break, he wandered off near her camper where the door was ajar. He heard her talking on the phone with a friend.

"I'll tell you, all these guys want from us girls is any kind of sex!" she complained.

The same cop told me that the lead singer from The Who, Roger Daltrey, said to him that Linda Eastman was quite the rock groupie before she married Paul McCartney; she was always snapping pictures.

True or not, there were many tales to be told. My guess, though, is that most of those fables, like many third- or fourth-hand tales, are closer to non-truths. It really meant nothing, anyway, because it was all useless information. Still, to listen to the stories of those who actually met these entertainment icons was heady stuff.

Scene V

By year's end, I had been assigned to the sets of Ghost and Awakenings numerous times. The excitement I felt about going to work bubbled over. This was the reason I loved movies so much. Yes, I did have thoughts about being a writer as well. I wished for a large book jacket to adorn the wall of Elaine's, the famous celebrity bistro that was more like a salon to many artists, thanks to owner, Elaine Kaufman.

However, it was acting that occupied many of my early fantasies. Picking up that gold Oscar statue would be a dream come true. Despite the disenchantment of my early longings, though, for me this job was great compensation.

***

One cold night in Times Square, we were sitting in a police car positioned right behind Robert De Niro and Robin Williams, who were in a New York cab that was being towed by a camera truck as a dialogue scene for Awakenings was being filmed. By the way, many automobile scenes from movies are filmed this way instead of the vehicle actually being driven. Towing the vehicle makes it easier for a shot setup rather than trying to situate a car following along with all the mikes and equipment. Those difficult shots are reserved for action scenes. I assume no one out there believes that Al Pacino drove the red sports car as a blind man in Scent of a Woman.

The director on Awakenings was Penny Marshall of Laverne and Shirley fame. Penny Marshall a director? Yes.

"Quiet! Rolling…"

On the evening in question, it was so cold that even the heat from the bright lights in the square didn't warm the air. There was no way that my partner, Officer Ganza, and I were going to stand out on the windy street, especially if we could get away with not having to do so. Sure, we should have stayed at our post and, certainly, production would have liked us to freeze just as they were. Many of them, including the director, were hunkered in heavy parkas, their breath creating fog puffs in the frigid air.

Our task was to direct traffic, but Ganza and I were in sync with a different scheme in mind. The older cops would never have faltered because they were too nervous about losing their detail, and they didn't enjoy our complaining. But we were young and sometimes foolish.

The hell with freezing! I thought.

We chose to follow closely in the warm police car and stick our hands out the windows when we had to stop oncoming traffic. Hey, it worked. Ms. Marshall, of course, was not happy. She fixed her gaze on us, and it was not with dancing eyes.

What the director then did, instead of voicing her displeasure to us directly, was notify the Mayor's Office of Film and complain about the lazy job we did.

"You guys aren't going to get too many warnings," our commanding officer informed us.

"But, Lou… "

"No, you listen! We'll all be toast," the lieutenant snapped, more in fear for his own cushy job. Luckily, we got off with a warning and, of course, the realization that we were expendable.

My movie career might be over before it started. Remember the rules and professionalism pamphlet?

"Do you think the Lou is gonna' dump us?" I would ask Ganza on several occasions.

***

I was fortunate enough never to be assigned to patrol in a full-fledged ghetto area, where neighborhoods were sadly depressed. However, I did work some interesting parade details and emergency mobilizations in such locations. Ghost was being filmed in many of Brooklyn's high-crime areas like Bedford-Stuyvesant and East New York, and I was assigned to work a few nights at that film.

During one of these shoots, I was privileged to meet the film's producer, Howard Koch. Mr. Koch was just hanging around the set, dressed in a long parka coat. He moved about with either a walking stick, or a cane; I couldn't really tell which. He always seemed to be gazing around, as curious as the next fellow who had never spent much time in this type of neighborhood.

Even members of the crew who were from California moved about wide-eyed; they actually asked us if something bad might happen around their precious set. I don't know why I was surprised; I thought they might have been used to working in crime areas, after all, didn't they have East L.A.? In our possibly dicey situations, they really appreciated the police presence. "Did you guys get any coffee?" was said with more fervor than usual.

So, as I was greeting him, Mr. Koch took me totally by surprise when he said that I had the look of an actor, not a cop. I was 5'8", no muscle mass to speak of, and probably 20 pounds overweight, but imagine the kick I got from his comment; here was one of the biggest producers in Hollywood — a stately man of great experience — complimenting me!

"You look more like an actor than a cop."

All I could muster was a shy, "Really?"

I wanted to scream with delight, "Put me in a movie, please! Knight me an actor!"

Mr. Koch also dazzled me with light conversation about an old film he had worked on starring John Wayne. One of John Wayne's best movies, The Searchers, also happens to be one of my favorite westerns of all time. Mr. Koch told me that the horse John Wayne used in that movie was actually his.

This guy is a big deal and a nice man, I thought, so I accentuated my smile and widened my eyes to give him a clear view of my baby blues.

Anyway, Mr. Koch never did put me in a movie.

In March 2001, this memory flooded back as I watched the annual showing of the Academy Awards—something I do every year, even getting up at the crack of dawn to watch the selected nominations. Although my experiences in the Movie Unit ultimately left me disenchanted with the whole celebrity-on-a-pedestal concept, in fact, I really had overdosed on idol worship and adoring fans.

However, I always loved this singular, most important awards show on television, even as I would eventually cease purchasing star magazines and periodicals. I had sworn off watching entertainment TV 365 days a year, except for the Oscars.

Although I tuned in with less interest than I had in the past, I still joined the ranks of billions wondering who would walk down the red carpet. The next day, the critics had a field day about length and boredom. On that particular March evening, I found the show to be lackluster and the interviews to be annoying and uncomfortable, even for the celebs, who seemed to be contemplating something else as they answered questions.

Still, we are a nation hooked on celebrity. Nothing new there. Worship of film stars by folks from all walks of life has been around since the days of Rudolph Valentino, when women fainted in the streets. Wandering aimlessly through the lives of those who are perfectly or imperfectly famous is the stuff of dreams. It's an escape from our own dull lives, and it serves as a timeout from the drudgery of our own shortcomings, family gossip, relationship problems, and limited finances.

For me, the one moment that stood out about that particular awards night was when the show honored deceased persons in the film industry. As the lights dimmed and the music went low in the hushed pavilion, John Travolta, looking every bit the movie star, walked somberly to the podium. He then gave a homily honoring those lost to the industry in the year 2000.

When the image of white-haired and distinguished looking Howard Koch appeared on the screen, I recalled the time when I had a front-row seat to the stars — when the man whose face on the screen before me had spoken those magical words of encouragement.

You look more like an actor than a cop.

Who knew that I would eventually be no longer enamored of celebrity culture? Who knew that I would have real responsibilities? Who knew that, in the September following that March night, the world would change forever?

*****

Now, I want to go back to the time when Ghost had taken on the ghetto. In the film, there is a scene in which Patrick Swayze fights with a foe. In the finished product, Swayze is seen punching it out with his nemesis, his punches going right through the enemy, because, well, he is a ghost. Of course, as they filmed the fight scene, Swayze is actually battling nobody. He's just punching harmlessly through thin air for the camera's effect.

Folks in depressed neighborhoods are just as enthusiastic about the movie experience, so, on this night, instead of being bothered by the weather, many of them braved the evening chill and eagerly convened on the set to watch the making of a motion picture. This was back in the late 1980s, when crime was high, but the neighborhood was peaceful on this ghostly evening. For whatever reason, the residents of Bed-Stuy took to calling Patrick Swayze by the descriptive name of "Patrick Swingy." I'm certain it was coincidence that Mr. Swayze was, indeed, swinging. So, as Swayze was doing his scene, swinging at the air and attempting to maintain his method, a cheer arose from the crowd of onlookers, and their laughter echoed through the set.

"Hey, Swingy!" "Shit! Look at Swingy!" "Who the hell is he swinging at?" "Go get 'im, Swingy!" they shouted.

"Quiet on set!" a PA bellowed, trying to drown out the catcalls.

Fat chance of that. Quite frankly, the production company was lucky that's all they heard. Swayze stormed off the set, obviously annoyed. There went my picture opportunity. We were asked if we could convince the spectators to quiet down.

"On their own block? In this neighborhood? I'd like to see you try!" I replied.

Many rules did not apply here, and there was no telling if production would ever get their shot, especially if the excited residents were asked to shut up.

"Quiet! Rolling...!" was a courtesy request in Bed-Stuy. This was a place where props were not needed; the broken bottles, stacked garbage, urine-stained alleys, and trashed streets were real. Push that crowd and the threat of violence loomed. Later that evening, Swayze came out to finish the take. It turned out to be a good scene in the film.

***

It was a different story when the cast moved to the Wall Street area. We had to rope off an entire city block down by the NY Stock Exchange because the crowds swelled as word filtered around the offices and high-rise buildings that Patrick Swayze and Whoopi Goldberg would be in the street filming.

There was a sea of suits and skirts swirling all over the place as workers spent their entire lunch hours standing behind police barriers just to catch a glimpse of the handsome Swayze and the funky Goldberg going through a number of takes in which all they were doing was walking up and down a short sidewalk in front of Federal Hall. I thought I would get pictures that day but, once again, the excuses that always lurked in the back of my mind came forth.

Oh, I'll wait until the crowd dissipates. Same haunting

nonsense.

During filming, one of our cops happened to be directing traffic right in the camera's eye. Somehow, he made it into the finished film, forever immortalized in Ghost. His partner, Officer Calhoun, missed being filmed because he was hanging out with the teamsters telling tales of his active police days. However, he fooled no one, he was a film buff at heart. A nice guy, he just loved reminiscing about patrol, so he missed his chance to be in "the pictures," as the old folks say.

Had I any inkling that this might happen, I would have slyly pushed the officer out of the way and volunteered for traffic duty, myself. At the very least, I would have tricked him into believing there was a huge gourmet dinner inside the hall so I could swap places with him. Heck, if I knew local cameras were around any of the sets, I would have had my family tape the news, even if I were picked up on film simply directing traffic for a split second, which, a couple of times, actually did happen on different shoots.

On that day of shooting, there were rumors that some of the female fans had offered their panties to Swayze, à la Tom Jones. Funny, a relaxed Swayze confessed to one of our officers that he couldn't believe the attention, because he had had a hard time getting a date to his prom.

Scene VI

The 1989 holiday season was approaching, and the nightmare of New York's brutal traffic was in full bloom. One day, it took me a half-hour to go one block in the hub of Rockefeller Center and, yes, I was blowing my car horn along with the rest of the ignoramuses.

The season brought a slight break in film productions. Apparently, the holidays created an affable attitude in civilians as well as in police officers, who usually took a break from their endless barrage of summons writing.

The usual stress associated with holidays and gift buying, coupled with the pressure and frustration to collect a decent photo array, caused my obsessive behavior to kick into high gear. It's important to note that it was a time in my life when every little fart bothered me, from the traffic, to the weather, to certain people. I would complain about life in general, but I was determined to enjoy my holiday with my family.

Oh, I had self-control on the exterior, but internally, a crisis could pop up like a bad penny and trigger a rush of adrenalin. I would worry if I left the house on a bad-hair day, or if I brushed my teeth thoroughly enough in case I ran into a friend and I had to hug or kiss them. It is an affliction I carry to this day. I was frequently distracted; on some days, I could walk the boulevard near my apartment to mail some bills or buy a newspaper, and my mind would be wandering as if I were in a trance. I would end up somewhere and not remember the journey.

There was the time that winter, when a neatly dressed older woman caught me snapping bills as I exited the bank to ensure I was given the right amount, and she then watched as I walked to the mailbox and reached my arm in as if the box were the proverbial cookie jar. How could I confess that I wasn't sure if I'd find my mail, or if it had gone down the chute and vanished forever?

At work, I started to obsess over failures, such as when a policeman friend failed to get us a picture with a celebrity.

"Oh, damn it!" he had said. "I can't believe I screwed that one up."

I couldn't believe it either, and that would be it for me. It would bother me for the rest of the day. That's how it went, and poor Christine had a lot to deal with as I shuffled back and forth from my everyday proclivities to my childish complaints about pictures and life in general.

I tried to relieve my tension by thinking in the NOW, the real world. I was staying far away from the past escapes of nightlife and booze, trying to understand myself and process a new me. However, self-discovery wasn't easy, and often my frustrations would cause me to run off at the mouth.

"I'm sick and tired of this!" or "I'm sick and tired of that!" I'd blurt out.

I got used to those obsessive feelings — those over-stimulations that lurked, dormant, in my mind until they leapt forth, momentarily forcing me to take a timeout from the world in which I should have remained focused.

For the time being, my obsession with all the movie crap was a pernicious way of filing away for yet another day my personal relationships with my girlfriend, my friends, and my family. Those around me could have said I was wearing them down.

***

In November, prior to the holidays and the start of 1990, David Dinkins was voted in as Mayor of New York City. He had the distinction of becoming New York's first black Mayor, and he did so by beating the future dictator of the city, Rudy Giuliani. The race appeared to be close, still, Giuliani did not stand a chance; it simply was not his time.

Deplorably and unbelievably, cops were still being shot. As the war on crack raged, drug busts were recorded in record numbers in the hope that it would soon come to an end. God bless the NYPD!

On a frivolous note, many police officers were still sporting cool mustaches and walking with a swagger, gun belts swinging and clanging on their superhero utility belts. They flaunted the idea they were blue magnets, capable of drawing anyone's attention.

Cops on TV were still all the rage, and now New York would have two series filming simultaneously in the Big Apple: True Blue, a show about brave Emergency Service cops, and Law and Order, which was about lawyers and detectives. The ongoing filming meant that, no matter what was going on in the city at the start of the decade, one constant was for sure, eighteen other cops and I were still secure in our detail.

True Blue was filmed primarily in an old storage facility on 116th Street between Pleasant Avenue and the FDR Drive. This area of Manhattan—East Harlem—held nostalgic significance for me because, not only was I born there, but also my family's roots were just two blocks west on 116th Street between Second and Third Avenues. A plethora of early childhood memories lingered in the back of my mind—leaning on windowsills, watching wrestling in Poppy's shoeshine parlor, drinking coffee soda, eating Charlie Rooster (Charlotte Russe) cakes, and listening to the stories spun by grownups and my older relatives, many of whom are now gone.

***

One afternoon, bored and hungry, I wandered off from the set of True Blue and walked by Mount Carmel Church, the fine relic in which I was baptized. Unfortunately, the church had fallen victim to crime over the years. I continued walking another two blocks south on

114th Street and came to the popular Italian restaurant, Rao's. Stepping down into the old-world eatery, my eyes adjusted to the dim light and I could see where the bar was situated opposite the quaint dining room, complete with checkered tablecloths that added to the charm of the place.

A fellow police officer who was assigned to the set for the day but who worked at the neighborhood precinct called down to me from the top step outside the door.

"What's up?" I asked.

"A word to the wise. You can't be in here. It's off limits to cops," he hissed.

"Why?" I asked.

" 'The Job' says it's a mob hangout," he replied. "Don't let any precinct bosses catch you in here."

Then he laughed when I responded, "Don't a lot of retired cops hang out here?"

Needless to say, we both walked away from the joint.

Another glimpse into my personal life would reveal that, around this time, I started becoming brazen, though unwittingly. I began to send to various magazines a bunch of human-interest short stories I had been working on and finally completed.

What did I know about the intensity of revision or the enormity of the competition? Well, for one thing, I quickly learned all about the sting of rejection as the negative slips poured in from both popular and unheard-of magazines that wanted no part of my work. Luckily, because I realized I was a novice at this endeavor, writing remained my secret, so no one had to know how it had progressed or regressed.

***

I remained preoccupied with my Movie Unit career; that adventure was still in its early stages. However, as fascinated as I with the business, I was already becoming less impressed with the industry folk. See, a cop is like a ballplayer in uniform. Like players in any team sport, men in blue are perceived as all part of the same team. Police officers desire their deserved respect.

I would soon learn that, in pop culture and, for that matter, even in the bustling maze of Manhattan, there was not the same sense of reward that we had enjoyed in the outer Boroughs.

The greetings from passers-by and the acknowledgements from the people in the movie world I was not hearing as frequently as in the past. I was still a part of the subculture of the NYPD and, in my heart, that is where my loyalty would always lie, even though "The Job" could turn its back on a patrolman in the blink of an eye.

Perhaps, because I was slighted once or twice, I'm blowing the whole situation out of proportion. Sure, not everyone was all that bad. The idea was that I had to learn to adjust to the attitude of my fellow officers in the Movie Unit.

"Be friendly to everyone. Don't take this shit seriously, it's just a game," they said.

Capezzio knew how it was played. So did Sorkorski and the rest of the guys, especially Officer Wallach, who had no interest in taking pictures. He just loved mingling with various workers around the set. Wallach was sick of patrol and was very happy to be a part of the Movie Unit. He was the typical Irish cop, except that he was attitude-free and anger-free, and that's why he was good for the Movie Unit. Wallach could drink a beer with anybody.

The truth is that an entire city of police officers would think it moronic of me to complain about such trivial happenings. Imagine if some had heard me gripe about not being able to get a picture with this one or that one? I chalked up my ridiculous feelings as being frustrated by the ultra-liberal attitude of both movie people and the wide variety of multicultural residents of New York, many of whom are not even natives of this city.

Most cops are naturally biased against extreme liberalism. Our political leanings are a little more conservative, starting with a thumbs-up for the death penalty, especially for cop-killers. Those who worked in Manhattan and in the movie culture were an eclectic group, and some of us felt that many of them overdid it in their quest for tolerant causes and ideas that I knew they wouldn't embrace so enthusiastically if crime were pissing in their own liberal backyards.

As a matter of fact, there were many celebrities who were advocates against firearms, yet they felt they deserved the right to arm themselves because of who they were. And, other than the blue-collar workers who knew better, many of the movie personnel looked upon the police as their private security guards.

"Can you do this?" "Can you stand over there and make sure…" "Can you close the street?"

Of course, in retrospect, it didn't matter. What they asked for was really what our job description mandated. How someone presented his or her problem had nothing to do with it. I should have remembered that it's just a game.

Once, during a Woody Allen shoot in Gramercy Park, I was standing on the corner minding my own business when a woman approached to inform me that one of the garbage pails on the street was overflowing and the waste was causing a bad smell.

In an imperious tone, she demanded, "What do you intend to do about it, Officer? It's overflowing and starting to smell."

"Absolutely nothing," I replied. Cops are entitled to bad days, aren't they?

I really wanted to say, "Lady, you walk everywhere. How would you like to get stuck behind a garbage truck in traffic and the hopper juice is just leaking out all over the sidewalk as if it were liquid shit? I know the garbage stinks, but I'm trying to keep my eye on that brownstone over there to see who comes out."

She walked away in a huff, which surprised me. Usually, they ask for a shield number to make a complaint. I should not clump together the obviously obnoxious people with all of the civilians we encountered, but I do lean on the side of cynicism.

Scene VII

I learned from my fellow officers the art of trailer watching.

"Always keep your eye on those doors," Capezzio told me.

"What?"

"You never know who will pop out."

So, every time a trailer door swung open, I looked that way. The morning Connie Selleca peeked out of her camper to call for an assistant, I was so close I thought she was calling me. The camper door had swung so wide that she had to reach and grab it. Of course, she also had to bend slightly, and she was dressed in a snug-fitting red skirt and light top, looking absolutely gorgeous. I heard a rumor that Ms. Selleca had some family members who were policemen, so I knew she was probably receptive for a photo op.

Please let me get a photo with Ms. Selleca!

However, since I was once again on a one-man assignment, I fell back on my old adage, which was "later," and wound up skulking off at the end of my shift too nervous to ask her. Chalk up another disappointment. Connie Selleca.

Obviously, since I did not possess the balls to ask Ms. Selleca for a photo, there was no way I was going to approach the volatile Sean Penn, who, a few days later, was on the set of his new flick, State of Grace, filming in Harlem.

***

A few of us were sitting in a patrol car across from a vacant lot near Park Avenue in Harlem. A young PA who had strolled over to say hello was leaning against our cruiser. We spotted Sean Penn walking away from the set on the lot, and he appeared to be in a huff.

"There goes Penn," I muttered, more to myself.

The PA spoke from the side of his mouth just before he sauntered off, "Someone's gonna' get drunk, throw up, then return to the set."

The film was packaged with a large budget, Penn was the star, and his tantrums would be overlooked. Supposedly, for his troubles, he was getting $2.5 million and some serious, ego-demanding perks that included bodyguard Chuck Zito, a real-life Hell's Angel. That man literally followed Penn right up until the camera started to roll, playing every bit his part as a tough guy. At the time, I thought it was quite possible that he was packing a gun. It was cold during the shoot, and Penn's bodyguard would walk around with an eyesore of a statement—a large, tasseled fur coat. I figured who needed the aggravation of even asking for a photo, since there was the distinct possibility of being turned away with an attitude. That rejection, of course, would have ruined my day.

***

After a couple of months in the Movie Unit, the number of pictures I had to show for my intended photo collection was zilch. Oh, I had a collection all right, a list of potentials that just kept growing. I actually had this weird dream one night in which a faceless cop, taunting me with laughter, would not allow me the use of his camera to take a picture with a celebrity. I was becoming more obsessive about missed photo ops than I was about the mounting rejection slips from publications. The rejections were out of my hands. The photo ops were at my fingertips.

Scene VIII

Blow the trumpets! Finally, on January 18, I got my very first photo. Ironically, actor Dennis Farina was a retired police officer from Chicago, and he looked every bit the cop, a guy with hard-boiled features. I have to hand it to Mr. Farina; he walked away from his job as a policeman after 18 years on the force, which would have left him only two more to go for full pension. Obviously, I would not have taken that chance, but Farina went for it and made a nice career out of acting.

That day, Officer Ganza and I were assigned to the set where shooting was scheduled in lower Manhattan in the area of the Criminal Courthouse. Farina walked over to say hello and, to my surprise, he recognized Ganza from a previous shoot and greeted him personally.

"Hey, how are ya'?" Officer Ganza replied, cool as a cucumber.

Farina was all smiles and invited us into the makeup trailer.

"Come on guys. I gotta' get some makeup on. We'll talk inside."

The trailer was nothing glamorous, it consisted of a few makeup tables and the usual bright bulbs affixed atop the mirrors. It was a quickly put-together room in the back of a rig. It looked as if it had been set up for traveling carnival clowns. Nevertheless, this was a major TV production, and it was the real deal.

The makeup crew plied their trade on Mr. Farina's face, working swiftly. Textures were applied to his rugged features, signifying that even men in movies had to be made up for the camera's lighting. While the makeup techs worked, we all chatted about the happenings in New York and, naturally, Farina inquired about how the police were getting on. Being an ex-cop, he knew it wasn't easy and hoped we were being treated well.

Once a cop always a cop. I thought.

***

That same weekend, I got my chance to snap some photos. Since this was the same TV movie that Connie Selleca was starring in, I thought I'd get another crack at photographing her. The crew was filming a scene in front of the Rockefeller Center ice rink. Officer Ganza showed up shortly after I did, so I confidently felt set up to go.

Unfortunately, Ms. Selleca had made her way back to her trailer in a different direction.

Still, the day was salvaged when I had my picture taken with the serious and distinguished actor, Ben Gazzara, and later with the diminutive actor, Paul Williams, who made us laugh because he was still wearing his makeup bib. He didn't take it off because he thought it would make the pictures more comical. It did. That was the kind of interaction I would have liked to experience with all celebrities.

Later in the day, when the shoot relocated, we received a huge and unexpected surprise. The crew had moved uptown on Madison Avenue for further sidewalk scenes, where many swanky art galleries are located. Production broke for lunch and, since Ganza and I were not that hungry, we decided to linger on the sidewalk, bullshitting and people-watching. It was cold, but not brutally so; still we wouldn't last long standing out there. A good cop should never get too cold, too hungry, or too wet.

Soon, a black limo rounded the corner. That was not unusual on the Upper East Side; we were as accustomed to watching limos as we were to watching trailers. The limo pulled in front of one of the art galleries about a quarter of the block in from Madison. Out hopped Bruce Springsteen and his wife, Patti.

"Shit, it's Bruce!" Ganza cried. "C'mon!"

They were the perfect rock star couple. Bruce looked scruffy in blue jeans and boots and Patti, sexy in boots, was wearing all black that accentuated her gleaming red hair.

We scrambled to catch up to them before they could duck into a gallery. Our goal was to catch the star away from any onlookers so he wouldn't feel so rushed to escape. We followed them into the gallery, and one of the curators, an elderly gentleman in a blue blazer, welcomed us into the lobby, thinking we were just two cops seeking shelter from the cold.

I was wondering what kind of art a rock star would be attracted to. Maybe avant-garde?

We began to pace, but waited patiently, anyway. There was no way we were leaving. I eyed the walls where fine art was displayed, but I couldn't tell the difference between an expensive painting or one scribbled in a nuthouse.

Finally, we heard the clatter of footsteps on the top stairway. We quickly exited the gallery, thanking the gentleman at the door. Then we positioned ourselves in front of the building, and Ganza readied the camera.

I was so glad that I wasn't the one who had to set the shot up. Ganza not only held the camera, he had the guts to do it and a baby face that benefited his approach. When "The Boss" stepped out of the gallery onto the sidewalk, Ganza wasted no time.

"Bruce, mind if we get a picture?"

"Sure. Anything for New York's Finest," Springsteen said.

It was a piece of cake. We were two gleeful cops getting photos with "The Boss." I wondered why we didn't get a picture with Patti, but it all happened so fast that I guess we weren't thinking clearly.

Ironically, it all turned bittersweet with Springsteen. A decade later, he would ruffle the feathers of police all over the city in dramatic fashion. This occurred during a highly publicized case in New York in which a civilian named Amadou Diallo was questioned by police on a Brooklyn street in the dead of night. When Diallo reached for his wallet to produce his identification, the undercover detectives, shrouded in darkness, mistook the wallet for a gun and fired at Diallo, hitting him forty-one times. Springsteen would make a national story of the case by recording a song that included the incident. He mentioned the forty-one shots numerous times throughout his song.

Winter eventually turned harsh and, while working the movie sets, it was not as easy to duck out of the cold as it had been when we were on patrol. Supervisors would show up on sets, and it would have been a mess if two of us were caught hiding out at the same time. Since I had already been warned about this once, it limited my options to warm up! However, if a bunch of us were assigned to the same job, we were able to split our time in order to secure some shelter from the elements, if for only a few moments.

I came to relish the days when production was slow in New York, and we would be assigned a warm radio car, thus allowing us to sit in front of a building where a shoot would be filming interior scenes. Sometimes, on really slow days, we were given the option to take the day off. Fortunately, interior filming also required registering for permits, so it helped to justify the existence of the Movie Unit.

***

Next up was a commercial spot for the Revlon cosmetic line. When I heard that, I thought I was going to be entertained by the likes of Cindy Crawford and Stephanie Seymour. The shoot was to take place in the tubular walkway that hovered over a street leading to the front of Yankee Stadium. The wind was kicking up around the big ballpark in the Bronx and whipping through the tube, thus creating a wind tunnel. Since the models were unknown to us, and they were running late, Officer Gorman and I decided to duck out for a while. We had to pee anyway, and it was always better to go in a place that would be clean, because the public wasn't using the restrooms at this time of year. We wound up wandering the hallowed grounds of Yankee Stadium.

Those were the days when the Stadium Security acknowledged our uniform in a friendly manner, allowing a couple of cops to enter that awesome baseball cathedral. Beforehand, I had tried to buy a disposable camera in a couple of the bodegas and delis that were doing business under the elevated train tracks. To my disgust, I had no luck.

However, not having a camera didn't bother me too much, knowing we were not going to run into any players at this time of year. Gorman was not a celebrity hound; he was more of a young, shy, retiring type. He was in the Movie Unit for convenience, and he never carried a camera.

Nevertheless, there we were, roaming unescorted through the underground into the locker room of my favorite team. Walking in, I immediately noticed the side-by-side lockers of Don Mattingly and Dave Righetti.

Wow, I thought, it's a big deal being in the same room that greatness inhabited.

It appeared that the two Yankees controlled the biggest space in the row of bench lockers. Standing there, awed, I was suddenly struck by the sight of Thurman Munson's shrine locker. The area of Munson's locker was cordoned off with thin tape and had not been infringed upon since the great Yankee's death in 1979. His uniform jersey, number 15, was still affixed across the top of the locker. Shit! Now I really wished I'd had that camera or that Gorman carried one. Instead, it became another Movie Unit disappointment for me.

I thought about Munson for a moment and remembered when he bestowed his kindness on my family by giving my dad, whom he called his favorite maitre d', tickets to one of the 1978 World Series games. It was my bad luck to be in California that fall, but at least my brothers and sister were able to go.

Along with other Yankee players when they were in town, Munson used to frequent my uncle's restaurant in Manhattan.

He always greeted my dad, whose name was Tom, with a big smile and a "Hey, Mr. T."

I remember when Munson was killed in a plane crash. My dad called to tell me the sad news.

After leaving the Yankee locker room, my partner and I walked through the dugout. From there, we strolled onto the field and out to where the plaques of the Yankee greats were proudly displayed. Then we moved back to the pitcher's mound, and I felt like screaming for joy. I marveled at home plate where Reggie hit those three historic homeruns on three pitches, a feat that will never be matched.

"Look where I am," I said quietly; but I wanted to shout it out into the whistling wind!

The cold weather was dug in; it remained a real New York winter with plenty of frigid air to go around. I thought in my off time that I would write more and maybe create a piece of work that would be really interesting. However, my ego was greatly deflated by the rejection slips that were coming in like junk mail.

I often thought, who am I kidding?

The one constant with rejection slips was that they came in the mail, and I didn't have to deal with face-to-face personal rebuff.

My girlfriend also had her work cut out for her as she continued listening to my constant and selfish gripes. I had everything I wanted except the ability to conquer certain mood swings. Why I had these ups and downs, I did not know.

I had moved into that stage of our relationship where it wasn't only about the romance. Yet, as in the past, I wondered if I had ever really lived life before settling down. I'm surprised that Christine didn't run for the hills. To my good fortune, she had foreseen a growing substance in our coming together. Although I was uncomfortable with being comfortable, there were moments when I knew it was right.

One such moment was the humorous fix we gave each other on the evening when I was feeling sentimental about throwing away some old plants that were lingering on the fire escape by my kitchen window. My display of what Christine thought of as nonsensical sentiment caused her to burst out laughing in an infectious, alluring way that caught fire for both of us. I don't think I ever laughed that hard with any other woman in my life.

Thankfully, movie assignments were coming in spurts. It was just too cold to have to be standing on a corner directing traffic. Still, the downside was that I didn't have very many pictures for my collection.

***

One morning, I was assigned to a commercial with another big Irish cop. We were just hanging around shooting the breeze when I turned and spotted Mary Tyler Moore standing in the doorway of a mid-block hotel. She was bundled up, a stylish scarf around her neck, obviously warding off the cold and waiting for the doorman to call for her car.

I grabbed my partner and said, "Let's go!"

All of a sudden, I had balls.

Mary Tyler Moore made it easy, because she was extremely cordial to us. It was a huge relief, especially for me, since I was the one who approached her, and because I was the one who would secretly have been crushed if she turned us away. When we snapped the photo, Ms. Moore seemed concerned that our fingers might have been blocking the lens.

"Take another one," she said.

The actress made me smile when she removed her glasses for the photo. Funny, I was wearing glasses that day, as well.

Of course, it was many years after her famous show, but, for me, Mary will always be that cute girl who worked in the newsroom on The Mary Tyler Moore Show.

That week, I anxiously waited to see the photo I took with Springsteen. The first view of the picture reinforced a worry that would haunt me for the rest of my Movie Unit career. Blurry, dark, or light photos are a nightmare with any picture, but, when they include a celebrity I might never come in contact with again — well, that was a whole different scene.

The Springsteen picture, even though the camera was held

in the steady hands of Officer Ganza, was clear, but way too dark. I even had the developer run it through again to lighten the shade. That didn't improve the picture. My obsession then kicked in, and I had them run the photo through again, and yet again. Unfortunately, the picture never did turn out the way I wanted.

Scene IX

What better time to escape New York than when it's dreary and cold? I decided to take my vacation time and go down to Florida. However, before I left, I got an important reminder of what it was like to be a cop. Officer DeRosa, who is an all-around nice guy, Officer Hubish, and I were assigned a quiet, late-night shoot on the Upper West Side, when suddenly we were approached by a frantic woman telling us there was a problem up the street.

"A man is running around with no clothes on! He has a knife and he's screaming! He's up the block," she shrieked, her arm outstretched and pointing.

"Oh, shit!" could have been said collectively, as we sort of slowly made our way to West End Avenue, hoping the nut job would have gone back inside from the cold. He hadn't. As we turned the corner, we immediately saw a huge black man, apparently high on drugs, running in circles screaming who-knows-what? My patrol instinct smelled fear, which is what happens when boredom fades and the sharp edges of anxiety and the sense of imminent danger take over.

Officer DeRosa was not a big guy; he was only about my size, but he was an experienced cop who had previously worked in one of the roughest precincts in New York. DeRosa approached first, his hand on his weapon.

When it was apparent the guy was not carrying a knife, DeRosa attempted to put the man at ease. Hubish and I remained on either side, brandishing our nightsticks. Somehow, and thankfully, DeRosa managed to convince the hyper, naked man to sit on a stoop.

We waited for an ambulance to pick up the EDP (Emotionally Disturbed Person) and cart him off to the nearest psychiatric ward. It was a godsend that we didn't have to attempt to subdue the subject. I mean, his pecker was swinging in the breeze, and I noticed his hands; they were almost the size of small baseball gloves. It would have been a nightmare for the three of us to cuff him. Dealing with the crazy effects of heroin can be a tough prospect.

Off to Florida, which gave me a chance to connect with my girlfriend, and spend time with my parents who lived down in the Sunshine State, and whom I missed deeply. I missed my mom and her pasta, and I missed watching TV with my dad.

It's amazing what a change of scenery and weather can do for the soul, far away from the NY concrete, although my thoughts would drift back to my job in New York, and I would secretly wonder who would be in my next photo. However, when in Florida, do as the natives do. We walked on the beach, swam in the pool, and enjoyed some fine meals in good restaurants. We also made time to take in a movie. Many people think it's a waste to use a night on vacation to go to a movie, but I relished it and appreciated that Christine recognized the small things.

Pictures anyone? On the flight back to New York, I noticed that the famous horse jockey, Angel Cordero, Jr., was on the plane. Christine had gone to school with Angel's daughter, and she had met the jockey many times. She said hello to Cordero and they exchanged pleasantries. YES! I saw a photo op!

When we landed, I asked Christine to quickly find the camera in our luggage bag.

"Are you nuts?" she exclaimed. "I will not embarrass myself!"

"You're right," I replied, and we both laughed.

***

I was enthusiastic about returning from vacation, eager for fresh start. Soon, I hoped, the harsh, gray winter would give way to the soft greening of spring. Unfortunately, New York was, as usual, damp and gloomy. Still, my post-vacation assignment was a good one. I was sent to Radio City Music Hall for interior shots. I figured it would just be a hang-around gig—maybe theater folks shooting a commercial. At least I didn't have to waste a day and take the night off or stand out in the damp weather.

When I entered the hall, I was surprised to learn that Officer Fontaine and I would be escorting musician Kenny G on a walk up the Avenue of the Americas. He would be playing his horn, sort of like a pied piper, as people would stop to watch him. The crew would also be walking with handheld cameras, and they hoped to get the shot in one take, since the skit was just a quick introduction to an Arista Records music special being held at the great hall.

While we waited for the crew to assemble, Officer Fontaine and I were treated to a pre-rehearsal of the show, where Barry Manilow and Jeffrey Osborne were practicing their turn in the lineup for the program. Other than a few production personnel and the music technicians, we were the only ones in the huge theater. It appeared as if they were performing on stage just for us. The sound of their voices resonating through the hall along with the acoustics and piano sent an unexpected chill through my artistic soul.

Of course, I had no camera in my pocket. You would think I'd have learned my lesson by now and carry the damn thing as if it were part of my uniform. What the heck was wrong with me? Officer Fontaine didn't normally carry a camera, so I was really disappointed.

Finally, we proceeded along the avenue with Kenny G and the crew. He was a friendly sort of guy who possessed a mellow demeanor that seemed to go with his long, curly hair. He embodied an image of a star who had no apparent airs, and he said hello to anyone who recognized him.

We walked the street under the lights of movie cameras and street lamps, and my artistic side found the experience somewhat enchanting.

Kenny was playing his sax beautifully, and we passed a group of homeless people who also seemed to be in a trance. No one was willing to interrupt the medley or spoil the moment.

A passerby, who just happened to be singer Neil Sedaka (YES!), stopped us. Although he didn't appear to know the musician, Sedaka hugged Kenny G and introduced him to his wife. When people are in a similar profession, it's like there's a kinship. (We cops are the same way.)

Officer Fontaine, who had a habit of whispering, even when he wasn't telling a secret, joined in on the camaraderie.

"Hi, Neil, do you remember me?" he asked, softly.

Greetings were exchanged all around, making Officer Fontaine smile broadly, because he and the crooner had once been in the same show. Meeting Neil Sedaka on the street must have been a nostalgic experience for him. Fontaine is a singer who had performed with the oldies group, The Regents. He is living proof that not all participants in the entertainment world are famous and financially successful. He remained a cop for 26 years, which certainly wasn't a bad second-choice career.

After the shoot, one of the production people offered to take photographs of Kenny G, Fontaine, and me. He said he would send them to us after he developed the film. We were both grateful that someone had a camera; however, we never did receive the pictures with Kenny G.

What's the matter with people? I thought. Why be courteous enough to take a photo and then not send it?

What an evening that would have been, four pictures. Instead — nothing.

I tried shaking off my failed photo-snapping experiences with the knowledge that four movie productions were rolling into town. And, whenever New Yorkers would pause to watch what they thought to be the glamour of movie-making, I would be right there, privileged, on the other side of the rope.

The streets were going to be bustling with film crews from The Bonfire of the Vanities, The Fisher King, Funny about Love, and New Jack City.

Scene X

The Bonfire of the Vanities was a massive production, with a multitude of hands, equipment, and hundreds of extras on deck. The shoot would require a number of cops for many of the crowded and equipped street scenes. The Department had to detail local precinct cops to assist us, and they were more than eager to catch the assignment. They, too, wanted in on the glamorous world of movie-making. Their presence would crimp our style a little, because it meant that more cops would be wanting photo opportunities.

Early on, we, the Movie Unit cops, were introduced to the movie's star, Tom Hanks. A number of scenes were shot on the grand ascending steps, which rise to the halls of the Bronx Courthouse. One shot in particular called for heavy rain. It was bright that day in New York, but the magic of movies was ever-present. With a heavy downpour of showering "rain," the crew transformed the dry Bronx pavement into a drenched street.

This rain-making magic was accomplished by means of huge water trailers carrying tons of water that was pumped through the sprinkling pipes that hovered over the street much like the crane arms of a giant erector set — it made me think of a huge, grownup toy. All this was done out of the camera's eye, of course. As the cameras rolled, the water showered from the sprinklers, creating rain that looked as natural as if it were really pouring from the sky. It is the genius of Hollywood to create illusion. The technicians can make rain, mist, fire, clouds, or freshly fallen snow, all to satisfy the movie-going public.

Later that same afternoon, our Movie Unit was introduced to Tom Hanks, and we took a group photo with the star.

We laughed when Hanks kidded us, " Da, da, da, dum, you SOD bastards!"

(SOD was the acronym for Special Operations Division, the Department umbrella that the Movie Unit fell under). Mr. Hanks obviously was informed about which cops we were, and he agreed to be in a good-faith photo.

Lou Goldman, a renowned newspaper photographer, snapped the picture, and he was kind enough to send each of us a black and white, 8 x 10 photo of the group.

Also on set that day, playing himself in the movie, was tabloid journalist Geraldo Rivera. Many cops I know believe the rumor that Rivera's real name is Jerry Rivers, and that he had changed it so he could further his career as a serious Hispanic journalist. I believe the gossip is false.

Continuing with a Geraldo rumor, a crewmember told us that the famed reporter almost slugged it out with Hanks's bodyguard. We never did find out what prompted the altercation, but it was certainly believable, given the attitudes of those bodies-for-hire. Geraldo is known to have had boxing training, so he probably could have given that bodyguard more than the bodyguard bargained for. Nevertheless, Geraldo was cool with the cops, taking photos, signing autographs, and wishing us well.

***

Down on lower Broadway, the film, Funny about Love, was shooting some sidewalk dialogue scenes. My partner for the night was my buddy and ball-breaker, Officer Sorkorski. 'Ski was also an experienced picture taker, and I'm sure his friendly nature had a lot to do with our success. His light features, blond hair, and welcoming smile always seemed to guarantee a smooth approach, usually resulting in handshakes from many celebrities. Boy, I wished I had his attitude!

Leonard Nimoy was directing Gene Wilder and Christine

Lahti in an attempt at romantic comedy. Officer 'Ski smoothly approached Nimoy and got one photo taken for me. I instinctively eyed Nimoy's ears, but they were not the size of a Vulcan's auditory appendages.

'Ski knew it was going to be too easy for me with him at the wheel, so he maneuvered a classic cut-up. He insisted that, if I wanted a picture with Gene Wilder, I had to be the one to ask the actor.

Oh, that 'Ski! I thought. He just loves the laughs.

He relished knowing how inept I was at approaching stars.

So, I worked up the courage to ask Wilder.

"Yes," he said.

Wow! I almost fell over. But wait, although he said yes, he just kept on walking. This appeared to be a backhanded rejection, my first. I was a little stunned. Sorkorski was hysterical — the in-your-face-joker kind of hysterical. I played it straight, but I was inwardly livid. Sorkorski busted my chops about it for the rest of the shoot.

Surprise! After the crew wrapped the last scene of the night, Wilder walked over to us. "Officer, do you still want that picture?"

He even asked if the building that I was leaning on was a good-enough background.

"Sure, sure!" I happily responded to both questions, and I breathed a sigh of relief at the retracted rejection.

I was so flattered that I thought about asking for an autograph. However, I always felt lucky enough to get a picture, so I convinced myself that it would be bothersome to Wilder if I asked him for an autograph. No, that's not quite true. In truth, the added stress of asking for an autograph would have killed me. Basically, I had ruled out asking for autographs right from the beginning of my assignment in the Movie Unit. All movie fans should be that considerate.

Anyway, Wilder walked away, leaving 'Ski with a case of contagious giggles.

It was inevitable that 'Ski would be there for another embarrassing and laughable moment. Once again, he would force me into doing my own bidding. We were planted on the busy sidewalk in front of The Plaza, assigned to a small commercial shoot.

"Watch some movie star come by and turn me down for a picture," I grumbled.

Suddenly, from a block away, I spotted Dustin Hoffman walking up the avenue. His steps were quick-paced, and he held his head straight up, sort of like Tootsie without the makeup. What came instantly to mind were conversations I had had with the guys who told me that Dustin was great with cops and an easy picture target.

"Please, 'Ski," I begged. "Ask for me. This is Dustin Hoffman we're talking about here!"

"Hurry up, he's coming," the imperturbable 'Ski responded. "Gimmie the camera, I'll set it up, but you stop him and ask. I handed Sorkorski the camera and nervously braced myself to ask the oncoming actor for a photo op. With extreme anxiety, I had my hand outstretched even before Hoffman reached me, and the actor obliged with a handshake as he rushed by. This was a very big deal for me.

"Dustin," I gasped, as I grasped his hand. "Mind if I get a picture?"

I don't know how it happened. Either Mr. Hoffman thought I was going to drag him off for a time-consuming photo, or he really was in a hurry, or maybe he just didn't feel like it.

He withdrew his hand from mine.

"I'm in a hurry," he said. "I really have to get to Mickey Mantle's restaurant to meet my kids."

I was beside myself. Here I had one of the all-time great actors right there in front of me shaking my hand and, like a fish flipping off a line, Hoffman was just—gone! Talk about disappointment. Disappointment made even worse by my partner's reaction.

'Ski was doubled over with laughter, mimicking me, "Hey, Dustin, mind if I get a picture?"

"C'mon, what happened?" I whined, all frustrated.

Then I just had to laugh along with him. The joke would linger in the back of my mind (and, I'm sure, in the back of many other minds) for my remaining time in the Movie Unit and even long after.

Anyway, my brothers in blue and I had nothing but time to continue cutting up on each other. On occasion, I would be taunted about my demure manner, which, by now, was regarded as my customary demeanor.

"Dustin, can I get a picture?" They mocked me in a falsetto voice, followed by bellowing laughter.

Then again, that's what cops did. We broke each others' onions. Jokes ranged from lighthearted digs to unmercifully cruel comments that only a police officer can take as a semblance of humor.

We even broke old Marvin's balls, a mind-his-own-business, old-timer who drove an old van that looked as if it were on its last wheels. We called the van "Marvin's Bus."

Sometimes, our attempt at humor would turn heated, albeit short-lived. Like many police officers, we were members of a cohesive group. Nothing was perfect, but we had each others' backs. Cops were not always friends, but we were comrades in arms, especially for safety's sake.

As for the Dustin incident, the only saving grace (I rationalized) that would lessen my obsessing over the missed opportunity was that the next day in the newspaper there was a brief blurb on page six that Dustin Hoffman was seen at Mickey Mantle's with his kids. At least he hadn't lied to me. Still, it was only a small consolation against the fact that I had no photo of him.

I was certainly passive, unlike the other officers in the Movie Unit. A couple of these guys elevated the photo-and autograph-collecting procedure to an art form. Some of them would immediately have their photos blown up to an 8 x 10 size, then get the photos signed by the celebrity on the next meet-up. These cops, though ballsy, also had in their favor the privilege of being privileged. They were in with the bosses as well as with the roll call cop, so they already knew what shoot they were going to get.

Officer Capezzio was the best, though. I swear he was the most obsessed fan I ever met.

***

Every day, almost up to the very moment when spring was supposed to be in the air (yet, the weather was still nothing short of dreadful), I was wearing my stupid, police-issued, long rubber raingear that looked like dull gray trail dusters.

One cold, drizzly evening, I was standing on the corner of Mulberry and Mott Streets assigned to another tedious commercial. The shoot was inside a storefront, so, feeling bored, I walked out to the corner to have a smoke. As I stood there in the light rain, a dark, four-door Mercedes rolled to a stop at the light. I didn't know it at the time, but inside the car was real-life Godfather, John Gotti. One of the teamsters later told me they had seen him get into the car a half-block away in front of a restaurant. A strange, irritating feeling suddenly came over me when I heard that. The most powerful, organized crime figure in New York had been sitting in a warm car wearing an expensive, dry suit, probably sharing a laugh with his cronies as they observed the lonely beat cop smoking a butt in the rain.

Later that same week, I was in Central Park, again standing in the rain and sweating under my rubber raingear. I hardly ever wore the raingear when I was on patrol, because there was always a place to sneak in and stay dry. However, this time, I had no such luck.

The zany Benny Hill was on set shooting a scene for British TV. His trademark bevy of heavy-busted women surrounded him. I asked Mr. Hill for a photo, and he graciously obliged.

He turned up his face and answered in his comedic kind of way, "Why, of course!"

It seemed that many of the comic types, like Paul Williams, Robin Williams, Danny DeVito, and Benny Hill, too, would usually act jokingly when asked for a photo.

On the same day, I got a cheesy photo with the friendly Lee Meredith. Ms. Meredith had made a career out of her chest, especially in Mel Brooks' film, The Producers. It is quite apparent in the photo I have with her.

Scene XI

It was a busy time and, next up, I was in Harlem for the film, New Jack City. The movie is a violent and gritty depiction of the drug crimes that were smothering New York. Judd Nelson, of Brat Pack fame, was goofing off on his sport motorcycle before the start of the shooting day. He was riding recklessly up and down the block without a helmet, although he was smart enough to tighten up his pants around his ankles. My first instinct as a cop was to go and break his balls. But, hey, I was in the movies now. It seemed to me that, besides the actual acting, carrying on was "it" for these guys. I must admit that I was a little envious because, quite frankly, they had it all!

We took pictures with Judd, and he jokingly quipped, "Hey, the last time I took a picture with New York's Finest, I was under arrest."

Then, for a moment, he sounded serious in his admiration for police officers. "I know," he said. "You guys really have your work cut out for you."

***

I was beginning to accumulate some pictures now, so I was camera-ready for my next assignment up around Central Park West. Green Card was a romantic comedy starring French actor Gerard Depardieu, and model Andie MacDowell. Peter Weir, of Witness fame, directed the film. Of course, we cops in the Movie Unit took photos with directors as well, so I approached Mr. Weir and posed the big question.

He greeted me with a demure handshake and said, "OK."

Gerard Depardieu was also on set, but, of course I dilly-dallied and, suddenly, he was gone. I didn't know it at the time, but later found out that the big French actor is huge in France. He is their Robert De Niro.

Quick Depardieu story: Officer Capezzio told me that he had taken a picture of the actor years before when he was not as popular. In the photo, Depardieu is smiling and holding a monkey on his lap. When Capezzio showed him the photo, the star began belly-laughing.

"You never know about the picture you're going to take," Capezzio told me.

Andie MacDowell remained on set after Depardieu left, as she required more interior filming. I couldn't tell if she would accommodate my request for a photo, because she had a natural appearance of being shy. Shyness, I believe, could cause unintentional rejection; on the other hand, I could just be rationalizing. On that day, the crew embarrassed her by wheeling out a huge birthday cake, right there on the closed-off street, and everyone, including me, sang Happy Birthday to her. Ms. MacDowell did oblige for a photo op. There was an innocent loveliness about her that was captured in the picture.

By now, it was apparent; the bigger the celebrity, the more nervous I was about my–approach. It was sort of like meeting a beautiful woman. The more beautiful....

It did not help my cause that I simply took bad pictures! 'Ski was a constant reminder of that fact, and he never missed an opportunity to tell our colleagues how my hand would shake as I held the camera, blurring every photo. He certainly knew, since he was the recipient of a couple of my mishaps. I snapped him in two blurred shots. One was a picture with Jessica Tandy, and the other was with Robert De Niro.

If any of the guys asked me to shoot a photo of them with a celebrity, I knew it was their request of last resort.

"Your hand shakes too much," I was told a thousand times.

***

Our next assignment was to work on a murder mystery, A Kiss Before Dying, starring the lovely, but perplexing, Sean Young, with Matt Dillon as her lover. We were assigned to 15th street in lower Manhattan when we approached Ms. Young. It was 'Ski who did the asking, and Ms. Young smiled and said that she wouldn't mind, but we would have to wait until after they shot the scene. Because they weren't close to filming at that particular moment, her response led us to believe that maybe all the tabloid stories of her flightiness were true.

We soon found out that her immediate refusal to wait was because she thought she was the one who had to secure a production person to take a snapshot for us.

"Not to worry," we informed her. "We have our own camera."

"You do?" she replied, smiling her pearly whites.

We took our pictures (even the one of 'Ski came out clear) and, for a good part of the day, we stared at and gossiped about Ms. Young's breasts, where her obvious high beams (nipples) were noticeably prominent under her transparent, shoulder-cut shirt. She looked so sweet as she glanced our way, and we were certain she knew we were ogling.

Matt Dillon arrived wearing dark glasses and a trench coat. He walked around aimlessly, and I didn't think he was dressed for the scene. We asked for a picture.

"Sure, but make it quick," he said. He was very cloak and dagger, as if he were a moving target, but I couldn't say why.

Yet, Matt Dillon turned out to be one of the nicest actors I ever met. He was a regular guy and would often come over and say hello to us, sometimes making small talk about our Movie Unit, the police, guns, the local nightlife, and the friends he had on the police department. My immediate thought was, wow, this handsome guy must score so many women!

***

The hit show that spawned a franchise began its long relationship with street filming in The Big Apple. The television show was Law and Order, and it starred Michael Moriarty, George Dzundza, Chris Noth, and Richard Brooks. Since the actors were usually always on set, everyone got photos with them, even civilians. Mr. Moriarty was really nice, and he exuded a calm and pleasant demeanor.

He was always saying hello, and once sincerely said to us, "God bless you guys!"

This was before 9-11, which made the comment all the more genuine (after 9-11, everyone blessed us — for a little while anyway).

On a corner in Tribeca, where Law and Order was filming a scene, Chris Noth walked over to say hi during a break. He looked like an actor, tall and handsome. Still, he was fairly new to publicity and the recognition game. He was obviously enamored with the sight of famous actors. Well, weren't we all? Remember, James Dean was in awe of Brando, and so was Pacino. Noth said to me that he had just seen Robert De Niro and Harvey Keitel crossing the street, chatting the entire time.

"It just blew my mind," he said, with wonder in his voice.

Law and Order would keep the Movie Unit busy for quite a number of years, thus balancing out the months when things were slow.

Scene XII

Pictures became a dangling carrot for me, especially when I got bored and my interest waned. Very early one morning, with crust barely out of my eyes, I found myself weary, standing in the quiet darkness.

What the hell am I doing?

I was assigned to Rockefeller Center in front of the statue of Atlas, who bears the weight of the world on his shoulders. It was sort of the way I felt at times.

I thought I was working touch-up exterior shots without actors present. It was strange to see Fifth Avenue and the sidewalks of Saint Patrick's Cathedral so barren. New York isn't always the "city that never sleeps."

This is this spot where I had once sat in traffic for what seemed like an eternity. I leaned against a light pole, and it was too early even for coffee. The city streets always take on a macabre, noir mood at this hour. Maybe it's the rank odor and the shreds of mist rising from the wet sidewalks that are hosed down each night by the building custodians as they wash away the grime and garbage, the layers of exhaust and, I suspect the piss — all the detritus that accumulates during the day.

On this damp, dark morning, campers for the film were parked off the corner to the north of the intimidating Atlas statue, which stood strong on the east side of Rockefeller Center.

I didn't want to hide out in my car just yet, because my book had not yet been scratched (signed) by a supervisor. That signature meant I had been checked on and present at my assignment. Like I'd be anywhere else at that time of the morning! So, there I stood, sleepily, on the corner, when I heard the sound of the camper door opening.

Bruce Willis stepped out, dressed rather nattily in a pressed white shirt, probably for his scene, and he walked the short distance toward me. I gave a quick glance over my shoulder to check out the person he was obviously walking toward. Uh, oh! There was no one else on the street. Before I knew it, Mr. Willis was in front of me smiling, his hand outstretched.

"How are you this morning, Officer?" he said, and we shook hands.

I was certainly not accustomed to a celebrity presenting himself to me, so, naturally, I was quite surprised. I mean, the most I ever anticipated was a nod. Of course, I was pleased to meet the actor. In situations like these, I probably could have engaged in small talk if the very concept of celebrity didn't intimidate me.

"Bruce?" I finally asked. "Do you mind if I take a picture with you?"

It's always about the photo op, and this appeared to be in the bag. I realized I had asked prematurely, because there wasn't anyone around to snap the picture for me. However, as soon as I thought about my situation, a teamster appeared out of nowhere. He could take the shot! However, I had forgotten to turn the camera on, so I nervously thought there was something wrong with it.

Mr. Willis laughed and said. "Don't worry, we can do it later."

I thought to myself, that's never going to happen.

I mean, is a star like Bruce Willis really going to remember to take a picture with me?

But he did come back after the scene, just like Gene Wilder had, and I got my photo.

Very, very cool!

***

A Kiss before Dying was in its last stage of exterior shooting.

It's funny that they shot many scenes around New York, but the movie's story line was set in Philadelphia. They even dressed up the front of a New York City Court building, covering the Court's name with a Philly logo. I can't see why they did it that way; filming in New York certainly could not have been cheaper than shooting in Philly. Probably it was more convenient, though.

We went up to Central Park West to relieve the Movie Unit's day officers. Nothing exciting. We already had pictures with Ms. Young and Matt Dillon. We were relieving one of the female officers, PO Muldoon, a nice girl from our Movie Unit.

She came up to us and said, "Hey, did you guys see what happened?"

How could we? We had just arrived. She explained to us that, apparently, a member of the cast in the film had to go to the bathroom, but there were no porta-potties set up around the set. The campers were also inconveniently parked at another location, so the actress, covered in her poncho, just squatted behind one of our police cars and relieved herself. I didn't think it was such a big deal because, as we all know, working outside and suddenly having to go could create a dilemma as we tried to scamper to the nearest bathroom, regardless of its decor. Not every restroom was as gorgeous as The Plaza's potties.

Scene XIII

As far as I'm concerned, any gangster movie that came after The Godfather was attempting to model itself on a film that could never be duplicated in its power and beauty. I was just fourteen years old when I first saw The Godfather. Subsequently, I read the book a few times over the years.

When I decided that I wanted to see the movie, my parents were very reluctant to allow it because my dopey aunt had seen it and described to my folks the film's violent and vulgar content. Still, they also knew that everyone in the neighborhood was going to see it, and enforced rules on ratings were not as strict as they are today, according to the viewpoints of many parents and theater management.

I believe my parents acquiesced because they rationalized that I was a huge movie fan, and that my older, wiser, and future brother-in-law, Tommy, would accompany me.

It was a mesmerizing experience. Even at that young age, I was left with a lasting impression that completely bowled me over and made me want more for years to come. The movie was every bit as good as it was cracked up to be. The moving, operatic style embellished larger-than-life characters who pulled me into the story immediately. The sheer scope of the movie was fascinating, and its visuals of rich, dark textures were stunning and unique for the time.

The Godfather abounded with colorful anecdotes — unforgettable lines of dialogue that were steeped in memory and recited in their own culture — repeated and mimicked in everyday life over the years by old and new fans, alike.

"It's not personal, its only business."

"I'll make him an offer he can't refuse."

"Bada Bing!"

The movie is a rare work of art; it's more than just a Mafia story, and no matter how many times it is viewed, someone, somewhere, will stop channel surfing and watch, if even for only a moment.

It all began with the writing. I revere the storytelling of author Mario Puzo, and I'd be lying if I said I did not wish to emulate that great writer's masterful style. I even took a writing course at the New School, an educational institute in New York that specializes in fine arts, because I knew that Puzo had attended that school in his early years.

It is extraordinarily difficult to conjure up a page-turning story — not just any story and not a quick beach-read, but a story rich in depiction and character — a story so grand as to be a completed work of art. Don't believe how difficult it is? Try it. I was very disappointed when some critics reviewed and dismissed Puzo's work as "airline travel pulp," or "eighth-grade reading level," whatever that means, because eighth graders should not be reading Puzo books — with one exception, his children's book, The Runaway Summer of Davie Shaw. Critics are sometimes harsh. They want everything to be brilliantly literate and to their personal liking, whatever it is.

Anyway, I prefer to abide by those critics who have given positive reviews to Puzo's work, claiming the writer to be a "master storyteller." Puzo, himself, once said that reading Dostoevsky changed his life.

I think reading Puzo has changed mine.

Still, gone are the days when one could waltz into a studio office with an unfinished manuscript, its draft wrapped in a brown paper bag, as was The Godfather.

Puzo is certainly not alone in creating the brilliance of The Godfather. The amazing artistry of Francis Ford Coppola comes alive on the screen as he portrays, with depth and sensitivity, Puzo's literary characters. Coppola's genius is forever ingrained in the moviegoers' psyche. Coppola is also no stranger to storytelling, as is evident by his

Academy Award credit for his screenwriting on Patton.

The Godfather is a film that consistently appears on most critics' all-time, top-ten lists. Naturally, the movie is a favorite of many antisocial people but, ironically, it is also the favorite of many federal agents and prosecutors, such as Rudy Giuliani.

Spring is a fabulous season for filming movies in New York. The sidewalks bustle with the excitement of a new film production. In 1990, the magical feeling of moviemaking was never more intense, because production of the long-awaited The Godfather, Part III was to begin shooting in the Metropolis.

That was what it was all about for me; it was the crème de la crème of movie making. I was like a sleeping bear awakening from a long winter's nap. Part III of my favorite movie, and the only book that I read three times, was about to be filmed here in New York, in my universe!

The buzz swirling around Coppola's third installment of his masterpiece fairly resonated in the air. Everyone involved in the New York film world was talking about the movie. Even as I was assigned to other projects, Movie Unit officers were talking about how this one and that one were working The Godfather, Part III, and how they wished they had been the ones assigned to the project.

Wracked with nerves, I wondered, would I get any time on the set?

In the meantime, I would have to be satisfied with the buzz from a distance. Rumors circulated around the film and its stars. Who knew where the tales came from? However, since I was enamored of gossip, I loved any hint of a story, and my ears were primed even more than usual to soak up juicy tidbits. Of course, with the tremendous hype, also came plenty of negative comments.

Age-old controversy raged about budget inflation. Well, that was nothing new to Coppola. The dire predictions proved accurate as costs went through the roof. There were accounts of contract disputes with some of the main players. There were knocks on the story line, and it was rumored that the script was doctored on a daily basis. There was concern that there might actually be three different treatments floating around by the time filming commenced.

In addition to those contentious issues, there were the famous casting problems. Robert De Niro's name was being tossed around for the role of Vincent Corleone, Michael Corleone's illegitimate nephew. However, De Niro had played Vito Corleone in The Godfather, Part II, so something just would not gel there. Correctly, the part was given to the wily Andy Garcia.

Many actresses' names were tossed around after Winona Ryder bailed out from Johnny Depp exhaustion; names such as Julia Roberts and Laura San Giacomo were mentioned. Coppola was stuck, but not for long. The director called on his real-life daughter, Sofia, entrusting her with the role of Mary Corleone.

Coppola's bold choice created an outpouring of negative sentiment throughout film land. Me? Hey, I had no problem with it, though I certainly thought Winona Ryder was perfect for the role. Robert Duvall, who played the loyal consigliere in the first two Godfather movies, was not loyal to the third project, opting out because the money was not right for him. His character was crucial to Pacino's Michael. So, if Al was getting $5 million, why shouldn't he? Enter the tan man, George Hamilton, as the new Corleone lawyer. Hamilton looks good on film, but he is no Duvall.

There were further rumors that Al Pacino and Diane Keaton were struggling through their own personal relationship. It was the second go-around in the love department for the pair, who had dated during the first Godfather film. Now, it was feared that their turbulent romantic woes would spill onto the set.

Who really knows? I mean publicists have always had a way of planting stories to create hysteria around a movie and attract attention.

So on it went...script...cast...locations...changes...changes... changes. Yet, with all the excitement looming, I had not been penciled in to work any of the upcoming shoot locations. I grew more frustrated with each day that passed, especially when I saw that the same cops were being assigned over and over again to The Godfather, Part III. I knew they were "in" with the roll call officer, and they would continue to be assigned to the film until they got all their desired photos and, finally, at their leisure, they would want to move on to something new. My anxiety increased every time I opened a newspaper and gawked at paparazzi shots of Pacino and company filming at various locations around Manhattan, from the sidewalks of Park Avenue to the old St. Patrick's Cathedral, which was a relic in Little Italy. Hell, this was film history, and it just did not seem fair that I was unable to relish the moment.

Didn't anyone realize what a huge fan I was?

I, of course, persistently hinted to the roll call cop, Spinell, that I should be assigned to work the film. How did I do this? I commented on movies and celebrities I loved, all the while hoping that he would not ignore my passionate interest. I even faked small talk with him about his passion, sports.

"Do you believe those Knicks?" I once asked him. (I didn't give a shit about the Knicks.)

It was bad enough that he had left me out of two previous productions, The Prince of Tides and Black Rain, but to not work The Godfather, Part III? It was unbearable!

Spinell couldn't care less. He just wanted to get those assignments out as soon as he could, so he could go back to his newspaper and bologna sandwich.

However pissed off as I was, I had to accept my fate. After all, this was still the Police Department, and I had to keep in mind that I was still a cop. The walls had ears and, if I voiced my complaint too often or blatantly begged, it would result in the opposite and spiteful effect. I was irritable, but my only choice was to hope that I would be assigned before production left New York. I was well aware that movies came and went quickly in the city, and I was running out of time.

So, I stayed at other jobs and was bored to death. There was a shitload of commercials and horrible rap videos starring so-called artists I had never heard of. Come to think of it, I never remembered much about the commercials, either.

Day after day, I stewed in my own lividness. One morning, on Centre Street, I had to work especially hard to keep my cool as I stood by a barrier used for the Law and Order set. I was thinking about how these freaking wooden barriers always gave us dirty, painful splinters.

Standing and waiting was now old hat. If I was asked one stupid question that day, I was asked a thousand.

"What?" "Where?" "How?" "Oy!"

I remained calm as I held up one of the barriers so a crippled woman could pass by. As I lifted the blue wood, a slew of pedestrians suddenly appeared from nowhere and scuttled through right behind the woman, barely allowing her to move out of their way. What rude morons people can be! But I just huffed and puffed. Without a cigarette.

***

Then, as if a bright spot had been specifically saved for a lovely May morning, I was given the assignment I had long dreamed of. I was to report to the corners of Prince and Elizabeth Streets where The Godfather, Part III would film the Little Italy Feast scenes.

I wanted to sarcastically stick it to Spinell, "Are you sure about that?"

I called Christine, exclaiming, "I got it! Tomorrow, I'm on The Godfather!"

I think she was excited for me just because she wouldn't have to listen to my bitching for awhile. Being assigned to work on The Godfather Part III was better than a trip to Disneyland. I wanted to call everyone who knew how in love with movies I was.

To understand my passion about movies is to picture this: a closed set where your favorite film is being created and you are invited backstage or off camera as an observer to the sequel movie's scripted scenes being shot for the first time. WOW!

I experienced the same kind of excitement that I had felt as a kid when I waited for Batman and Robin to get off the bus on Main Street. Now, I wanted to see the stars who made the Corleone family come to life.

It didn't matter to me that my report time to the production was 0500 hours, otherwise known as 5 a.m. non-military time. I was astounded that I got the assignment, and I was so excited that I barely slept that night. I could wander around like the walking dead in mid-afternoon on a music video; but this was going to be heaven, even at dawn. Lack of sleep didn't worry me, because my adrenaline would keep me wide awake, as if I were jacked up on coffee.

Bright and early the next morning, wide awake with anticipation, I snatched the keys off my kitchen table as if I were a bird swooping down on a worm. Hurrying to my car, I hit the early morning open roads. The promise of my assignment caused me to speed as if I were late for a party. I couldn't wait to get there.

When I arrived at the location, I spotted Officer Ganza. It was a cool morning for May, but I couldn't care less. The whole thing was unbelievable. The teamsters and movie crew had already staged the set to look like a real Little Italy festival.

How great is this? I thought.

Ganza and I walked to the craft service table that was set up with bagels, coffee, and assorted quick snacks. Ah, another smorgasbord of junk food! I fixed myself a cup of coffee that was a bit light, not the heady blend one would whiff in the early morning from the top of the stairs at home. Coffee served in white Styrofoam cups was never as good as coffee poured in a Greek-designed plastic cup.

As jazzed as I was, I felt unnecessary pressure, not only because of my obsession to get photographs, but also because I was thinking I had to live up to my Movie Unit reputation of easily brushing elbows with the stars, so to speak.

"You know, I met so and so..."

And, when I finally would see the movie, I could say, "I was there."

In retrospect, I'm sure nobody really cared.

A few of the teamsters—construction crews, electricians, and truckers—and many of the production assistants were making their way to the craft services table. The production assistants had been up all night braving the spring chill, setting up traffic cones and securing the parking for permitted production cars and trucks. They certainly needed the coffee.

"Hey, Officer, what's up?"

"Hey, guys," I replied. "What's up with you?" I'm waiting for Pacino.

The teamsters were more like us than the movie crews were. They were blue-collar workers who just earned a lot more than we did. They drove and unloaded trucks, constructed sets, and hauled cable.

I was holding my cup of bitter coffee, when I turned and saw actor Andy Garcia shaking hands and saying hello to a group of workers. Garcia looked very bohemian in a black beret and sunglasses. He was friendly and obliged anyone who wanted an autograph and a photo. Of course, Ganza and I got in on the action.

Nervously, I asked, "Andy, mind if I get a picture?"

"Sure, Officer, no problem."

It was great to see a celebrity acting like a regular guy.

"I'm surprised you asked all by yourself," Officer Ganza snickered, good naturedly.

"You're right," I replied, laughing. "I don't know what got into me."

We were sharing a joke with one of the teamsters, when the chitchat was pushed to the back of my brain as I focused my attention on the trailers, which were the temporary residences for actors, directors, and producers. Most were run-of-the-mill rigs—the type used by traveling families. Celebs used them as hiding places where they could relax between takes.

I was looking for Pacino.

Moments later, a whale of a camper slowly and ponderously pulled up, and we were told it was director Coppola's private trailer, the old, but redesigned "Silver Fish." It was filled with state-of-the-art equipment that he could use to review the film right after a scene was shot.I tuned back into the conversation.

"Boy, would I love to see the inside of that," I remarked to Ganza.

The young teamster chimed in, "That Coppola is some character, getting that whale all the way from California."

The teamster, it turned out, was chauffeuring Coppola from his hotel to the set. I asked him the usual questions.

"What kind of guy is Coppola?" and "Does he say much?"

The young driver replied, "Coppola appears to be a heavy thinker."

I figured that all directors must be heavy in the thinking department, actually. Then the driver told me that, on the previous day, Coppola was sitting in the back seat smoking a joint when he mumbled to the driver, "There isn't much loyalty in the film business."

Was he thinking of Duvall?

I imagine that disloyalty in the film business is quite true, despite all the accolades and gushing "thank you" speeches recited on award shows.

After a few minutes, the teamster driver walked off to go and pick up the director.

I was left wondering about Coppola, a proven talent who had given the studio two previous masterpieces in The Godfather, Part I and The Godfather, Part II, not to mention that he made instant celebrities of the cast.

Pondering the teamster's remark, I wondered, did Coppola still not have full control of the movie?

As day began to awaken, we were told that others would be appearing on set. I was nervous that the day would fly by. Ganza then wondered off to say hello to some of the crew members he knew and also to call his girlfriend.

I was smoking a cigarette when, moments later, a station wagon pulled up to the curb. Out hopped the famous director, himself, Francis Ford Coppola. I was curious about why he arrived in a car, not a limo, but that turned out to be a teamster regulation. Celebrities who desire to travel in limousines or any other kind of transportation still have to pay the teamster wage on a car and driver. So, not surprisingly, many film people opt to be driven in a car.

Coppola immediately ducked into his luxurious private camper. Finally, he emerged, dressed in a rumpled, pastel-colored suit. Battling my nerves, and without my partner around, I threw caution aside and seized a photo opportunity. I grabbed a nearby production assistant to do the honors with my camera. When the picture was snapped, Coppola noticed that the flash went off, and he suggested that it was unnecessary to use a flash in the early morning light.

Always the consummate director. I thought.

As we finished taking the snapshot, a fan happened by on his bicycle and asked Coppola for an autograph, which he gave, borrowing my pen to sign the excited fan's dollar bill. Though it was the perfect opportunity, I adhered to my rule of no autographs (in the end that would prove to be foolish because I would have had a rare collection). However, I knew that once I had one autograph, I would be compelled to collect many more. No need to up the stress meter! I did think about saving my pen that Coppola had used, but decided that honor should be reserved for Presidents' pens.

The day wore on, and Ganza was still nowhere to be found, when the ex-middleweight champ, Vito Antuofermo, wandered onto the set. Vito certainly looked the part with his pugilist appearance, his trademark flattened nose, and his hard face under a head of tight, wiry hair. Vito had a small role in the movie, playing a Mafia bodyguard called "The Ant." I asked him for a picture, and he was happy to oblige. The guy accompanying the boxer was a stereotypical Italian with distinct hand mannerisms. Wearing a dark leather jacket that enhanced his tough-guy image, he strutted up to me and started bugging me about a parking ticket he had just received.

"C'mon, can't you take care a' this thing?" he whined.

His argument was that Vito was nice enough to pose for a photo.

"C'mon, you got your picture!"

Yeah, right!

I mean, even Vito didn't bother me about it. But the extension of celebrity thinks it can reach anywhere. There were degrees of separation, I suppose, although it didn't help the boxer's friend.

Judd Hirsch, of Taxi fame, walked through the set saying hello to various crewmembers he knew from previous shoots. I was on a roll and quickly asked the actor for a picture. There were plenty of crew members to snap one for me. At first, Mr. Hirsch didn't hear me, or perhaps pretended he didn't, but, uncharacteristically, I pestered him. I was getting aggressive at this. Mr. Hirsch finally agreed to take the photo. I now had four pictures in the bank, and the day was not over yet! I believed that somewhere on the set was the elusive Al Pacino, and I was determined to get a photo with him.

As the first shot of the day was about to commence, the crew and the extras were moving into place. It was part of the Feast scene with the suave, but not pretentious, Joe Mantegna, right in the middle of things. The extras in the shot were to react to the sound of gunfire by screaming, shrieking, and ducking in and out in unison, acting as if they were in total shock and surprise.

Watching Coppola work behind those wondrous movie cameras was nothing short of magic. It took me back to my high school TV class when the teacher would show us old reels created by master filmmakers like D. W. Griffith. On late assignment, Officer Wallach showed up and, just in time, my partner, Officer Ganza, reappeared from his long break.

A curious crowd began to form on the outer perimeter of the roped-off set. I spotted Tony Bennett standing in the crowd of onlookers. I grabbed Ganza, and we nonchalantly made our way through the crowd toward the singer. Officer Wallach stayed back; he wasn't as dogged about getting snapshots. He would take the photo for a brother officer — no problem — but he would not be the pursuer of pictures.

As we approached Tony Bennett, we moved in sync with the people, because we didn't want to create the false impression that we were after someone for an arrest. The old pro, Ganza, smoothly approached and secured for us a couple of quick snapshots. Tony looked exactly like he did on TV, flashing those pearly whites through his crooked smile.

"Thanks, Tony!"

As it turned out, straining to see Pacino was a waste of time and eyeball energy; he wasn't even on the set that day.

"Did you ever get a picture with Pacino?" I asked Ganza.

"Yeah, yeah. Don't you remember asking me that before?" he grunted.

"Yeah, I remember. I guess I'm just hyper, thinkin' today was gonna be it for me." I sighed.

"He'll be back," Ganza reassured me. "He's always in town filming something or other."

Still, I was satisfied with a great day of successful picture-taking. When I called the office at the end of my tour, I was told to report again the following day to the same location. I was elated and could hardly wait for today to pass into tomorrow.

***

The next morning, I was back on Elizabeth Street to work The Godfather, Part III. Two days in a row! How lucky was that? From one of the production assistants, I got hold of a call sheet, which is a shooting schedule for the day ahead as per production. The call sheet also lists the characters and cast on hand for that day. Pacino was not on the call sheet, but it didn't mean that the actor wouldn't show up. The director might call for a change of scene.

Rumors were flying that real-life Godfather, John Gotti, might make a brief visit to the set. Gotti's social club, The Ravenite, was just around the corner from the shooting location. Where else but in New York could two Godfathers, one real and one celluloid, converge within a block of each other? However, neither "Padrone" showed that afternoon.

There were more of the Little Italy Feast scenes to be filmed with actors Andy Garcia and Joe Mantegna. Mantegna was cast as rival mob boss Joe Zaza, who was at never-ending odds with Garcia's character, Vincent Mancini.

"Be happy to," Mantegna replied when Ganza and I asked for a picture.

The actor also mentioned that he was elated to be in the film because he thought the movie was part of film history. Years later, he would narrate an audio edition of the original novel.

Here I was, an Italian-American cop, surrounded by Italian-American actors, on the set of the quintessential Italian-American film, shooting a sequence at a realistic Italian-American feast. I felt so cool that my spine straightened.

The feast, carefully designed to be a faithful replica of the real San Gennaro feast, was complete with colorful food stands and carts where the delicious aromas of sausage, peppers, hot yeasty breads, zeppoles, and other delicacies wafted into the streets. Italian flags, their red, white, and green bars dazzling in the sun, adorned the neighborhood fire escapes, and echoes of native accents could be heard. It was better than the real San Gennaro feast, which was always so crowded. Production actually hired legitimate vendors to cook and bake cannolis, all of which we happily consumed. I had my camera tucked in my back pocket, hoping the main man would show today. Once again, I was looking for Al.

Andy Garcia was back, and he was filming a scene in which he was on horseback on a side block adjacent to Elizabeth Street. An experienced trainer was assisting the actor, who was practicing atop the horse. The horse was huge and, I believe, it was borrowed from the stables of the NYPD. Horses do not come any larger than those of

New York's Finest. In addition to their imposing size, police horses are bomb-proof, not startled by the environment.

With Garcia regally mounted and riding up and down the block, I inconspicuously snapped a couple of photos from my hip. Some paparazzi I would make! My foolish self-esteem issues brought the usual wave of embarrassment. I don't know why; it's not as if I'd be if I were caught picking my nose.

Funny thing: Garcia on horseback was a huge scene in the film. In the movie, when Garcia pulls the reins to make the horse stop and the camera closes in on him, he is actually sitting on top of a ladder, holding reins-to-nowhere in his hands.

Afterwards, I took a page from the Coppola fan and asked Garcia to sign a dollar bill made out to my girlfriend, Christine, who admired the actor. Good thing autograph hunting on that day was easy going, because I'd obviously relented from my pledge not to ask for autographs.

The next day in The New York Post, there was a paparazzi shot of Coppola carrying his director's chair. Ironically, it was another photo I had thought about snapping. Of course I did not. It was funny, though, because I didn't see any of the paparazzi lingering in the area. I guess I was preoccupied by the activity and blinded by the stars in my eyes. It sounds silly, but it was pretty cool to see the picture, knowing that I had been only a few feet away when it was taken.

I became obsessively familiar with the tabloids and the entertainment shows, and was always on the lookout for stories and photos of New York filming.

Even the local news channels were filled with entertainment news. However, not all the reporting was positive. There were many complaints from resident New Yorkers.

"Why do the bridges have to be closed down at that time of day?"

"Why does the street have to be blocked off?"

"What an inconvenience!"

Perhaps the streets were not bustling with the same excitement that I felt. And even now, when I open a newspaper, though it is a different time with many newer and younger celebrities, I still get a little thrill — and perhaps even a twinge of envy — knowing I was once a part of it all, where some of the biggest stars in the world filmed on the sidewalks of New York. Like many things in life, the good memories outweigh the bad.

In retrospect, I think I became frustrated working in the Movie Unit because celebrity was like a drug to me. Instead of just enjoying the ride, as my fellow officers suggested, I was stressed out all the time, as I worried about the pursuit of photographs, the hope of attending a wrap party, and the desire to amass a great memorabilia collection.

In many ways, I failed from the get-go, letting everything get to me — the photos, the assignments, the locations, the traffic, the crazy schedules, and the boredom. Instead of using the time to my advantage, I constantly surveyed who was on the set. It was an unhealthy focus, causing me to miss out on the conversations of my fellow officers — their words drifted, unheard, in one ear and out the other.

Since we are on the subject of parties, let me mention a really cool thing that some production companies do for their crews. After shooting is finished, they throw what is called a wrap party (wrap, as in "that's a wrap!"). It's what the director shouts at the end of each shooting day. How much money remains from the budget determines the lavishness of the event. Usually, some of the cast will join the crew at the party and, often, members of the NYPD are invited. If budgets didn't allow all of us to attend, then our do-nothing supervisors would steal our spots. I was still apprehensive about attending such parties because I thought if I missed an opportunity to mingle, it would be apparent that I had no balls. I felt that I had to network. I was also afraid that I would spend a perfectly enjoyable night out gawking at the door all evening waiting to see who would walk through it. I would feel compelled to ask for pictures from anyone who was somebody and, since I would not be in uniform, it could set me up for rejection, which, in turn, would cause me to have a bad night, anyhow.

Unfortunately and ironically, the one party that I really did not want to miss was the one I had to forgo, the party for The Godfather, Part III. The entire cast and crew reportedly attended, but real life took over reel life. My father lost his battle with cancer that same week; obviously, I was in no fantasy-movie mood.

Instead, I spent my time reviewing over and over what could have been with a dad I was not entirely close to until near the end of his life.

That same week, Frank Sinatra cancelled one of his shows because his long-time pal, Sammy Davis, Jr., had died. My father was in good company. Since I have mentioned Sinatra, let me pass on a little piece of film irony. It had long been rumored that Frank Sinatra was contemplating the part of an aging don. However, the role in The Godfather, Part III went to Eli Wallach. I found this strange for two reasons. First, after the book and movie for The Godfather were released, Sinatra wanted to beat the crap out of Mario Puzo for modeling one of the main characters after him. Sinatra even reproached the author in a restaurant and berated him in a room full of astonished diners. Second, back in the 1950s, Eli Wallach had originally been up for the role of Sal Maggio in From Here To Eternity. That role, of course, eventually went to Sinatra, and the crooner picked up an Academy Award for best supporting actor.

When principal shooting ceased on The Godfather, Part III, I knew there would be nothing to compare with the experience of hanging around that set, though, of course, I was disappointed in not meeting Pacino or Puzo.

So, we know that the original Godfather was an original and instant classic. The Godfather, Part II was equally successful and brilliantly complimented the first movie. Both films won Best Picture at the Academy Awards. Film buffs had been screaming for sixteen years for the continuation of the Corleone saga. Feeling the pressure and offered huge sums of money, Coppola finally agreed to resurrect the Machiavellian, Michael Corleone.

The Godfather, Part III opened nationwide on Christmas Day, 1990. Early reviews were not kind to the movie and, though it broke a Christmas Day record, eventually The Godfather, Part III was not a huge hit at the box office. On the big screen, the movie had its entertaining moments, but there were scenes that appeared choppy and rushed. With so many plot twists, anxious viewers would need a second viewing to grasp much of the story, preferably at home and away from the increasingly noisy theaters.

Coppola did some patchwork for the home version that was released later, but I still fantasized about changes in the film that I had dreamed up in my mind's eye. I especially wanted to see those characters who were missing, such as the extended blood relatives inside the Corleone famiglia.

Garcia was wonderful as Vincent Mancini, although the whole illegitimate-son storyline rang false and without merit.

Unfortunately, when I saw the film in the theater, there were many rude distractions from moviegoers; although, in retrospect, the scenes where the audience members were laughing were some of the dialogue clips that could have been revisited. However, since I was a huge fan of The Godfather, I did find the third Godfather movie to be entertaining just because it was, well, a continuation of The Godfather series, so to speak. I must say, though, that the flawed movie did leave me yearning for more.

No, The Godfather, Part III is not the masterpiece that The Godfather and The Godfather, Part II are. Producing a movie of equal quality certainly would have been an historic accomplishment. As a fan, I was glad there was a third installment; however, I can't help but wonder what might have been. I thought Coppola and Puzo should have nailed it.

Scene XIV

In early June, filmmakers were again fortunate to be treated to some fine New York weather. As for the NYPD, they were hoping the summer would bring positive reviews for their beefed-up Community Officers Patrol Program (CPOP). More cops than ever were being assigned foot patrol in order to bridge the gap between the police and the community. Having been there and done that, all I was interested in was movies and their stars.

Robin Williams and Jeff Bridges were still around town managing to finish up some sequences for their film, The Fisher King, which, by the way, was a very relaxed set, especially when compared to the over-publicized, big-budget productions where most of the crews appeared tense.

Dressed in character as the street vagrant, Robin looked so natural. He often fooled the many passersby who wouldn't recognize him if he walked up and shook their hands. He was a pretty friendly guy, always saying hello, so, when we requested photos, it was no problem.

He even joked that, because he was in costume, "This will be a good picture."

Both Williams and Jeff Bridges were always smiling, and they looked as if they were just regular guys who were comfortable around the set and mingling with the crew. To me, that was always impressive.

One afternoon, Gary Busey visited the set to say hello to his pal Bridges, so my cohorts and I grabbed him for a group shot. In that fleeting moment,there were just too many of us to get individual photos.

Mr. Busey said, "I learned a lot about cops and police work just by doing movies."

***

I was drinking a soda on a warm day while hanging out on the sidewalk of Central Park West by The Fisher King set, when New York movie critic, Joel Siegel, happened by. It was always great to see someone in the public eye stop to watch the sidewalk filming, just as an ordinary fan would.

With my keen eye for spotting faces, I noticed Mr. Siegel and immediately asked him for a picture. After The Godfather, Part III, I was getting better at asking people (other than my fellow officers), to snap off a shot for me. Civilians usually lent a helping hand, but we rarely used the public for this little task in the fear they would want a photo themselves, and that could have been a pain in the ass.

"Sure," he said. "But call me Mr. Siegel, not Mr. Shalit."

Shit! Mistakenly, I had referred to him as Gene Shalit, a similarly featured New York critic who worked for another network. Hey, they both wore glasses and sported mustaches.

Anyway, Joel Siegel laughed and reassured me, "Don't worry, Officer, it happens quite often."

Oh well…

Contrary to rumors that would surface, The Fisher King was not based on a real-life vagabond who went by the moniker, Radioman. Radioman was a loner who looked like a vagrant. He would often show up at movie locations mounted on his old Schwinn bicycle — that model with the big wheels, sloped fenders, whitewalls, and wide crossbar. Dressed in black worn-out clothes, he sported an outdated kitchen-counter radio around his neck as if it were a large, bulky necklace.

Although Robin Williams resembled Radioman while in character, he was no match for the real thing. I mean Radioman was quirky. How this guy would find out where filming was taking place was beyond me. But anything is possible in New York. Many of the production companies were alarmed when he showed up, fearful that he was stalking celebrities, especially the most famous.

He was heard muttering on a few occasions, "Where's Pacino?" or "Where's De Niro?"

(Hey, we also muttered the "where is?" phrase.) Watching Radioman prowl around the set grumbling and asking questions of no one in particular was spooky stuff, I suppose, if you're a big celeb who's always concerned about unstable stalker-types.

However, Radioman was checked out, and it was determined that he had committed no crimes and was not considered to be a dangerous presence. Therefore, he was permitted to view a movie set like any other New Yorker, as long as he wasn't disruptive.

Radioman's persistence paid off for him, which I'm sure was enough to satisfy his motives. No, he did not achieve movie-star status, but he did receive his fifteen minutes of New York fame. To anyone who noticed, he would surface occasionally in the New York tabloids photographed in the celebrity sections sitting on his silver bicycle with the flared fenders, wearing that big bad radio around his neck. It looked like a bulky bib tucked under his scruffy beard. On occasion, Radioman would even get a celebrity on the set to pose with him, as Robin Williams did while dressed in character. It must have been a great shot—two characters.

Radioman is still out there on the New York streets patronizing movie sets and asking for Al. Watch those New York films closely; you might spot him in the background.

***

Before summer, more photo ops came my way. Fortune also shined on some lovelorn movie fans. Three Men and a Little Lady was shooting uptown near the American Museum of Natural History. Barriers were set up along the side of one building to hold adoring fans at bay and out of arms-length reach of heartthrob Tom Selleck.

Well, there are some days when everyone is entitled to a surprise. Selleck decided to approach the blue barriers. Then, leaning across them because he is extremely tall, he walked along the throng of very lucky admiring ladies, kissing each one of them. Witnessing these women of, ahem, "mature age" swooning was amazing. They were giggling like schoolgirls.

Also on set was Selleck's costar, Steve Guttenberg. When I had my picture taken with Guttenberg, I asked him if he remembered a certain neighborhood house party that took place in L.A. about 13 years earlier. Of course, I didn't expect him to remember me, although I was there at my neighbor's party, but he did remember the young lady who was the hostess, because a friend of his was dating her. He also threw out the name of the street she lived on, so I knew he really did remember.

My partner for the day was Officer Hubish, who really wasn't into the whole coparazzi thing. Nevertheless, she was a curious female who was eager to get her picture with Tom Selleck. Cop or not, she was an attractive lady, and the picture would look good on her wall. As we made our move to get the photo, Selleck's bodyguard, sensing our approach, asked us to wait because the actor was going over a page of the script.

No problem, because I knew that working with a female cop we were more than likely not going to be denied. While we waited, our sergeant paid us a visit, and we hoped he wouldn't stick around. The NYPD didn't want us harassing celebrities, so we didn't want to chance our boss spying on us, although if the boss wanted a photo, that would be a different story.

"Do as I say, not as I do," has always been the motto of the bosses in the NYPD.

Luckily, Sergeant Nedor was in a good mood: he asked about the shoot, spotted Selleck, Guttenberg, and Nancy Travis, and lit up his pipe. Finally, he walked away with his, "Look I'm working," clipboard in his hand, so we once again turned our attention to Selleck, who was in the midst of going over a scene. When he was finished, he walked over to us and we got our pictures with no problem.

"It was my pleasure," Mr. Selleck said with that rich, rumbly voice and handsome smile that caused my partner to blush.

"Next, I'd like to meet Van Damme," Hubish said, happily.

Shooting for Three Men and a Little Lady wrapped early, so the office reassigned us to First Avenue by the 59th Street Bridge where The Bonfire of the Vanities was shooting a scene with actress Melanie Griffith, who was being prepped to run across the street. According to one of the young production assistants, we had just missed seeing Brian De Palma, the director, put his hand on Melanie Griffith's derrière. Anyway, it began to drizzle, so production cut its day short, and I had to settle for a return wave to the one that I had sent out to Ms. Griffith from across the street. Her waving back to me made my day.

***

The comedy action film, The Hard Way, began its production run through the Big Apple.

My first day on set I was fortunate to get pictures with both stars, James Woods and Michael J. Fox. A bonus shot was with Fox's wife, Tracy Pollan. All three were accommodating, although Michael and Tracy were a little on edge because they were receiving death threats from an unknown psycho who gave no reason for his harassment.

Between takes, the pair was hustled off to their camper by their nervous staff.

The film also cast a few character actors whom I recognized from various movies and television shows. For some reason, as most unwitting thoughts just happen, it began to dawn on me that day that it felt weird witnessing all the actors in their natural roles as themselves. I began to worry that the magic and mystery of movies might slip away from me if I stayed too long in the Movie Unit.

Naturally, to most movie buffs, celebrities seen only on the screen and never in person are an enigma. Even when I would read about them, their images would remain undefined because what I read was simply words. It was quite different from seeing them up close, living and breathing. Over the years when I watched actors perform in a movie, I could separate my curiosity about and my interest in their real lives, and enjoy their interpretation of the character they were playing.

In my youth, the characters, especially, influenced me with their mannerisms and dress.

For instance, after watching Serpico, I began wearing a pea coat and Army jacket as well as a wool cap perched high on my head, just like Pacino. But, at my young age, I was unable to grow the beard. Meeting great stars when I was working in the instantly evoked memories of when I was young and truly believed that the whole idolization thing was for real.

***

The Hard Way was fast paced and introduced me to the world of dangerous stunts. In one scene, Michael J. Fox is supposed to accidentally flip the police cruiser he is driving in midair. Of course, the real driver in the scene was a stuntman. No sense in risking Michael J. Fox's life! The stunt was to be filmed on the West Side Highway piers. The stunt crew had decided to shoot the scene only once because of the risk, so there was a great deal of preparation.

The stuntman and the stunt coordinator had a great deal of conversation back and forth about setting up the whole maneuver, then the "driver" was buckled up and padded in. Essentially, he was boxed into place with many safety gadgets attached to him and all around him. The moving car was shot from a certain distance, so the stuntman was unrecognizable on film. The viewer would have to believe it was Fox driving that car. Well, because of the magic of movies, the viewer would believe it.

I, like the rest of the crew, watched with great anticipation as the car sped north on the pier until it hit its mark, a tightly built ramp that propelled the cruiser into the air, causing it to flip completely around and land back on its wheels. Everyone "oohd" and "aahd," then rapidly got out of the way, not knowing where the vehicle would eventually come to a stop. Fortunately, it stopped shortly after the landing, and the stuntman emerging unharmed to the crew's whistles and cheers. It really was outstanding, amazing, great movie stuff, and pretty damn brave, too! Michael J. Fox didn't even have to be on set for that take.

Officer DeRosa worked with me a few times on the set of The Hard Way.

One day, when we were discussing actresses, DeRosa turned to me and said, "The way you elaborately describe each of these women, are you sure you don't want to be writer?"

Actually, I was going through a patch where I had concluded that my writing was flat.

The following Saturday night, Christine and I went to Radio City to see Frank Sinatra. It was the first time I had seen the crooner perform live. Though he was past his prime, I still found his smoky voice and legendary cool to be marvelous. At a young age, to the dismay of my friends, I listened to Sinatra. A lot. When we driving around, I would slip in an eight track of Frank's music in between tapes of rock and disco. When it played, all I heard was groans from my pals. However, for me, Frank Sinatra was simply the embodiment of cool. If I could be like him, all the girls would love me. Let's face it, for all my talk about acting and writing, who wouldn't want to be a blue-eyed crooner serenading all those lovely ladies?

A footnote to the above: To become a police officer, a cadet has to create an entry psychological profile. One part of the screening process is to have the candidate draw a tree and a person. I didn't think twice before I drew a man dressed in a tuxedo with a cigarette dangling from his lips.

Hey, I passed the test.

There are times when I would have liked to live in a different era, like the early sixties, when President Kennedy once said the only other person he would want to be, other than himself, was Frank Sinatra. Sinatra is one of the great iconic personalities of the twentieth century.

Believe me, it would have been my biggest dream to meet him while I was in the Movie Unit. Yet, in a way, I was glad that I didn't, because the stress of trying to get a picture with him would have been huge. Heart-attack huge! What if I'd had the opportunity to be in that situation and catch Frank in one of his infamous moods, and he refused? I would have been crushed for life. Better to leave Mr. Sinatra on his pedestal.

However, I did get to see the crooner up close when I was younger. Once. After high school, I briefly settled into the family business. It was a natural progression to follow in my dad's footsteps and work for local 702, the union for line jobs in the motion picture film laboratories. Tucked in huge lofts in various buildings around Times Square, these laboratories were where the actual film stock for theatrical release was processed and shipped.

There wasn't much tape back in the 1970's, but there were mountains of 35 mm and 16 mm stock. The big companies were Technicolor, Movie Lab, and Precision. I would eventually work for all three. For me, it was the next best thing to being in the business, as were the years later.

My job title at the movie laboratories was Film Expeditor, which really meant "film-can carrier." I carried or transported by hand truck the large round film canisters that housed the stock. Day after day, I would push the loaded hand truck down lonely warehouse corridors in that maze of a film plant, as I delivered the cans of film to the various departments — chemical mixing, splicing, and delivery preparations.

There are so many elements involved in the big picture that go unnoticed. Hence, the forever rolling credits at the end of a movie, thanking everyone from the gaffer and his electricians who systematically set up and hide wires and cables, to the PAs who do just about everything demanded of them, to the truckers and teamsters who drive and unload trucks, to the best boy and his lighting crew, and even to the craft services caterers who make sure everyone is well fed.

However, every able body working under the umbrella of filmmaking takes a back seat to the stars, because they are the draw. They are the ones who sell tickets. Just about everyone who watches award shows does so only to see their favorite celebrities, not the boring editors or sound technicians, nor even the writers who dreamt the whole damn thing up to begin with.

The film labs I worked for housed mini-theaters or screening rooms, so that producers, directors, and actors could view what are called "daily rushes." The rushes were film taken from the camera on the day of shooting to be analyzed. In was in the "daily rushes" that decisions were made. Is it necessary to reshoot some of the scenes?

Occasionally, in my can-carrying travels, I would see a celebrity roaming through the building. In those days, I really didn't have the nerve to bother any of them. I was also quite short, and I couldn't see too far over the cans I was carrying. Once, when I was working at Technicolor, I almost stepped on Woody Allen's feet! De Niro used to pass through, as did Danny Aiello. Kirk Douglas was having lunch at the Movie Lab diner one afternoon, and I watched as he graciously smiled and signed autographs for a group of adoring ladies. I noticed that he had really big hands. The hands that wanted to hold his brain in Detective Story.

Then, there was the Man, himself. One day, I was waiting for the elevator in the lobby of the Movie Lab building on 57th street. When the elevator doors opened, I couldn't believe my eyes. There, stepping out, was Frank Sinatra and his wife, Barbara. They had been screening the day's shooting of the movie, The First Deadly Sin. Accompanying them was a huge bodyguard, who looked ready – almost eager – to crush any annoyance whatsoever.

Time slowed down for me; in my altered state of high-anxiety consciousness, they all walked by as if in slow motion. I was so nervous that I backed up into the wall with all the gracelessness I possessed. Sinatra didn't notice, nor even glance at me.

I was surprised at his lack of height; he was shorter than I imagined, yet, in a way, he was a giant. I continued watching as they exited the building and climbed into the back of their waiting car, a four-door maroon Cadillac.

I, of course, not being a police officer yet, did not posses any armor to brave an approach. I'll never know how Mr. Sinatra might have reacted. Instead, I would relive that moment in my mind for many years.

***

Away from reminiscing and back to reality: it was just another day, another shoot, or actually the same shoot, different day. One of The Fisher King stars was Amanda Plummer, daughter of great actor, Christopher Plummer. On the set, Amanda was always either in character or naturally zany. She was very nice, but flighty.

I was about to have my photo taken with Jeff Bridges. We were standing next to each other waiting for the picture to be snapped when, from out of nowhere, in stepped Robin Williams. He grabbed my arm.

"This will be a good one!" he said, enthusiastically.

Hey, hadn't he said those very words once before? He was right. That picture is one of the most natural photos I have.

Jeff Bridges was something of a camera buff himself. He frequently carried his own camera on set. He was said to be taking nostalgic shots of his experience filming The Fisher King. I imagine that he was also photographing his entire New York filming experience. Years later, Bridges published his book of photography.

The Fisher King wrap party was a casual event held at an attractive café/pool hall in SoHo. I was a decent pool player, but opted not to get involved in a game because I was interested only in gazing at the door wondering who would walk in next. It turned out I wasn't one for networking. Bridges was the only big celebrity who attended. I noticed him standing by one of the pool tables, and I grabbed Christine, who was reluctant, and we went over to get our photograph with the star.

Celebrities, no matter how friendly they might be during a chance encounter, will never remember the average Joe. Hey, it's even daunting for me to remember everyone I meet. That's why I often refer to many of my implied sources as "this person." I have crossed paths with movie people in Los Angeles, in the Movie Unit, the film labs, and on the street. How many people do you think a celebrity encounters?

I am certain that the sight of each picture I hold in my possession would trigger absolutely no memory of it being taken in the mind of the star who was standing next to me.

**

I am going to flash back again to the 1970s and another party I attended in L.A. I must admit that I was quite inebriated. In that state, I was inadvertently eyeballing a couple of girls sitting on a couch in the far off corner of the room. I could barely make out their faces. There was a guy sitting with them who apparently did not like the way I was staring in their direction, so he shot me some awful looks. I glared blurrily back at him, but nothing came of it. In retrospect, I realized that LeVar Burton might well have been itching to pick a fight with me, but he apparently thought better of it and stayed put on the couch.

Then, a dozen years later in the Movie Unit, I got assigned to the set of Burton's PBS kid series. Burton is always riding a cab in the show, so of course, the shoot was located downtown in an old taxi garage. Burton and I were discussing the weather when I got a picture with him.

He was actually a pleasant guy. I asked him about L.A.,

but avoided mentioning anything resembling a long-ago potential confrontation that had fizzled before it began.

Funny — first I met Steve Guttenberg, and then I saw LeVar Burton, both in L.A., and, years later I crossed paths with them in New York. Of course, neither remembered ever running into me. If they weren't who they were, I'm sure I wouldn't have remembered them, either.

During the Burton shoot, he was supposed to back his cab in and out of the garage driveway, which he did a couple of times. Recklessly. I laughed.

This type of double encounter would occur again sometime later when I encountered an irate Peter Boyle.

Scene XV

I was never going to be as capable and aggressive as my fellow police officers in the picture-taking department. That much I knew for sure. However, in conversations with my fellow officers, I found that they, too, harbored regrets over the have and have-nots over the years.

The great cameraman himself, Officer Capezzio, told me when he was on the set of Taps, he took a photo with Sammy Davis, Jr. Later, Capezzio realized he forgot to put film in the camera. It drove him nuts. He said that one incident bothered him for years.

It was also Capezzio who advised me, "Never assume that a bit player, or someone not as recognizable as the lead, might not someday be a major celebrity."

Capezzio had experienced this a few years back while working on a small, low-budget video. He thought at the time that the girl starring in that video was nothing more than a Madonna imitator.

So, he decided not to take any pictures that day. The artist was Cyndi Lauper and, from then on, Capezzio would take a photo with just about anyone who would stand in front of his camera.

Actually, the same thing happened to me, in a big way. I was assigned to a very low- budget film that was shooting in a desolate building in Williamsburg, Brooklyn. The day was dreary and damp, a perfect backdrop when going for dismal exterior scenery. I didn't even feel like being there and thought about telling the office that the crew definitely was not coming out for exterior shooting, so this way I would volunteer to go home. I spent most of the day sitting in my car, but then I had to go to the bathroom. I climbed the rundown staircase in the old Brooklyn walkup to the second floor, where the flimsy interior set was staged. This was, indeed, low-budget; the craft service setup was the size of a portable TV table, which also meant there would be no buffets on this shoot.

After attending to my business and too bored to go back to my car, I wandered around the bleak set. Sheets and blankets, instead of doors, divided dressing rooms, makeup rooms, and offices.

I made my way into a makeshift production office where an assistant was sitting at a desk. We were conversing about the business a little, discussing the negatives of low-budget productions and such. The talk soon turned to acting, and the heavyset assistant told me that he was an actor and that, on his last trip to L.A., he was able to snag an interview with director Oliver Stone.

"It was very uncomfortable," he told me. "The man just sat there staring into space and taking phone calls between one-word answers. He was rude."

Needless to say the assistant never heard back from the Stone people.

After that conversation, I moseyed up to the small craft service table. Not enticed by stale bagels, I took a chance, grabbed the last apple and leaned against a wall, since there were no chairs around. As I turned, I spotted a young man who, I assumed, was just standing there waiting for his instructions. The odd thing about him was his style. Dressed in what appeared to be 50s-style, glossy clothing, sort of what Elvis would wear, the young man looked kind of silly. He was sporting a huge, exaggerated, blond pompadour. Obviously, he was an actor dressed for his part as a rock star, or someone similar.

As I mentioned, this was a closed set with no personal assistants around to get in the way of a photo opportunity if one were to arise.

Photo op with whom? I wondered.

In all probability, no one. There were no celebrities around, and I doubted this kid was even close. The movie was Johnny Suede. The actor standing next to me, whom I decided not to take a picture with, was Brad Pitt. The same Brad Pitt who would become the number-one movie star in the world and the number-one requested guest for the Oprah Winfrey show.

Thelma & Louise was still in the editing process, and Johnny Suede was Pitt's first starring role.

***

It was just another humid morning, when we worked another lackluster assignment—a soup commercial in Alphabet City, downtown. I was already thirsty and uncomfortable.

Still, I was not terribly upset, because I was thinking about the book project I was about to begin. I certainly had no clue about the incredible amount of work that goes into the beginning of a project and seeing it right on through to the end.

Quite a few years and many revisions later, I would eventually finish the book originally entitled, Don't Let the Bear Eat You. Of course the book was about police officers. Anyway, I would receive many rejections from publishers. I had to accept the hurtful conclusion that my book was obviously an amateur production.

After much thought about beginning my writing adventure, I decided to find a pay phone and call the office to learn my assignment for the following day. The roll call officer was not the one who answered the phone, thankfully.

"Hey," Officer Ganza said.

He gave me my assignment, then said, "I'm headed your way. I have a still shoot with Eric Clapton in a building down by you in Alphabet City."

Holy crap!, I thought.

"Call me, call me when you get there."

"Yeah, I will, don't worry," he replied.

"Don't forget, call me!"

After Sinatra and Pacino, Clapton was "it" for me. I just loved the guy—especially during the 1970s when I was a teen listening to him through my space-like headphones. He was the guitar God whose pictures adorned my wall during those crucial years. By listening to his stirring guitar playing and his deeply emotional lyrics, my attitude toward love and loss was developed and defined. I spent countless hours playing air guitar to his music.

Ironically, I had just seen the man in concert the previous April at Nassau Coliseum. I went with a few childhood buddies, and it was the first concert I had been to since the 70s. All in our thirties now, we loved it even more and, on a new level, we appreciated the sounds of our youth.

The concert was filled with new songs from his latest album, Journeyman, a classic in its own right. In addition, Clapton indulged the audience with enough golden oldies to excite our memories and recapture those important times of our youth.

On Eighth Street, the soup commercial production had now become an annoyance, and I counted the minutes until Ganza would be arriving only a few blocks away. Finally, after what seemed forever, the commercial went to interior shots and, instead of notifying the office, I shot over to where Ganza was.

This was not the first time—nor would it be the last—that I abandoned a set in the quest of celebrity. I was still nervous, because if I were to be caught absent at my location, it would be extremely tough to explain. Yet, in times like these, I was so excited that I was going to meet one of my idols that it was almost worth it to get caught. That's what I was here for.

Police were not usually needed on still shoots, but our presence was justified because of the permits required for production. The crews would not be the wiser, because they were used to seeing the police around sets. Quickly, I arrived at the building and found Ganza. Surprise, surprise! Officer Stein met me and explained the scene in the upstairs loft. Apparently, Stein, a big rock and roll fan, had also skipped out on his assignment to meet the guitar god.

Ganza had a hatchback and in the trunk lay three outstanding electric guitars. Ganza and Stein (one of the most Bob Dylan-type, mellow police officers I ever met) were both into playing the guitar, but these instruments were Ganza's, and he was obviously as eager to meet Clapton as I was.

"Gonna get 'em signed!" he exclaimed, with all the excitement of a little kid who was getting a Radio Flyer sled.

"I'd rather be here than with a broad today," he quipped.

When we got up to the loft, the three of us each carrying a guitar, the production people caught on and were grinning at the sight of three star-struck uniform cops in possession of electric guitars.

Clapton was sitting in a back room on a soft white sofa when we entered. He was decked out in white Italian-made pants and vest for the shoot. He laughed along with his assistants when we entered. The atmosphere was unexpectedly casual. Clapton had no problem signing the guitars for Ganza. I told him that I had seen a performance of his Journeyman tour and thought that he was the best.

With his slow cockney accent, Clapton replied, "You really think so?"

He then took photos with us, and I even asked for his autograph (hey, he is on my top- three list!).

"Hurry," Clapton said, "I have to meet someone."

It turned out that he was in a rush to meet a friend for lunch. However, even though he was in a hurry, he decided to quickly strap on one of Ganza's guitars, and he began strumming. My two buddies followed suit with the other guitars, and Ganza immediately asked me to snap a photo. This was the ultimate in excitement for my cohorts and me.

We were all happy and satisfied with our brief interlude with one of the greats. Spending a few minutes with Eric Clapton and working on the Movie Unit sure beats walking a foot post with the weight of our belts carrying all the police-related hardware and not knowing what was ahead of us.

Later, Ganza blew the photo up to poster size and, when I saw it proudly displayed on his apartment wall, it appeared that Clapton was actually jamming with the cops. When I took the photo, every fiber in my being was obsessed with one thought—change places, and quickly, with one of the cops, and get yourself in one of those photos. Sadly, my passivity won again, and I had to settle for the one standard shot I did get. To me, this was logged as a failure because I regretted blowing that moment for a long, long time afterwards. My inability to get myself in a photo with Clapton was analogous to the Capezzio story of no film in his camera, only my story was of the cop with no balls.

Now, I realize how trivial that sounds, but I was in the Unit to capture some shining moments on film. That is serious business for a fan, and not a whole lot of people get that opportunity. It was sort of like being a paparazzi for oneself. But, like a kid, I would have to experience lofty triumphs and crushing disappointments all over again.

For me, shaking hands and meeting Eric Clapton was like pitching a near-perfect game. It was a photo, yes. Two outs in the ninth and the great photo was out there in front, ready for spontaneous capture. Instead of simply strapping on a guitar and striking a congenial pose, I spoiled the perfect game.

***

A few weeks after the high and low of Clapton I was told that a couple of stuntmen had been filming a chase sequence for the movie One Good Cop, when they wound up in the frigid East River off the FDR drive when their motorcycles went just a little too far and flew off the bulkhead into the drink. Thankfully, neither was hurt, nor were they subjected to treading water for too long, as they were successfully rescued to the gleeful cheers of the onlookers. The incident made the newspaper, and I recognized them from the news photo. They were the two stuntmen I had previously met, and the three of us had posed for a picture together. It is a relief to know that they are still among the living. Movie making is not without peril!

Stuntman Sonny Lee was a true Californian; he was in splendid shape, and his hair was bleached sunny blond. He was also something of a police buff. In his photo, he wanted us to show him with "New York's Finest slapping the cuffs on me." We happily obliged, and it was a delightful shot. It was always fun when the person is a fan of the police.

The other stuntman, Phil Tan, was built like Bruce Lee. As a matter of fact, he told us he was up for the part of Kato in a new screen version of the popular television series from the sixties, The Green Hornet, which starred Bruce Lee. I never heard about that film again, although I don't know why. Every other TV series of old was being redone for the big screen. You had to admire these guys because they had real balls.

The lead actor in One Good Cop was Michael Keaton, so, naturally, he was on set often. He played — what else? A New York cop, which was a far cry from Batman.

***

Summer in New York was hot and humid, and the city was worse for the wear. It seemed that crime might be on the rise, and there we were–cops simply watching actors portraying cops.

***

I went on a brief vacation to Lake George and spent quality time with Christine, my brother, and his girlfriend, Theresa. I needed to concentrate on personal relationships. We took in some sun, walked around the small-town streets after dinner, and just all-around relaxed. I stayed up late into the night that weekend to catch Frank Sinatra perform on the Jerry Lewis telethon.

When I returned to work, I was assigned to work outside the old Jack Dempsey bar in Harlem. Michael Keaton was there, and he was relaxed and friendly as he took photos and signed autographs for passersby. And for me. I know, I know, but I had to get his autograph for my nephews who enjoyed Keaton's Batman movie. Under his name, he very kindly signed "Batman" for me. I mean, Batman was a huge movie, and Keaton was just so cool.

Keaton was also a big Pittsburgh Pirates fan, and he was often seen sporting the Team's official logo hat.

***

Another afternoon, One God Cop was shooting in the old 84th precinct; the stationhouse was abandoned, so many productions would pay for the use of the old building. Visiting Keaton that day were three Pittsburgh Pirates, who were in town to play the Mets.

Bobby Bonilla, Andy Van Slyke, and Jay Bell all appeared to be thrilled to be watching the process of movie making. They obliged us with pictures and autographs (again, for my nephews) and especially for Officer Capezzio, who, since he lived in Brooklyn, went home to retrieve baseballs and a bat to be signed by the Pirates' hitters.

"Make sure you beat those Mets," I said to Van Slyke.

"I guess you could do without them?" he asked.

"I'm a Yankee fan," I answered.

***

From Manhattan to Brooklyn, then up to the Bronx, my trusty camera was as important as ever.

In Manhattan on the Lower East Side, Bill Murray was walking to the set of What about Bob? He strolled very nonchalantly, as if in another world. I asked him for a photo, and Mr. Murray gave a wry, comic glance into the camera. We shook hands, and I thanked him.

***

During the filming of One Good Cop, Stallone walked by the

set, and we grabbed him for a photo. No, it wasn't Sylvester; it was his brother, Frank. Hey, he did a few movies, too.

***

Suddenly, summer fled. Its passing was quick and lacked excitement. Perhaps many in the film industry were on vacation. I was still looking for Al Pacino to film something, anything, in New York. I was beginning to wonder if I would ever see him.

Then, one evening, when I least expected it, as I made a mad dash from the West Side to the East Side, and arrived at the New York University Medical Center, I finally caught up with the screen legend.

I was assigned to a New York University student film that was shooting on Columbus Avenue. My partner, Officer Williams, ducked out for a coffee break while I paced around, finally planting myself against a mailbox to smoke my umpteenth cigarette of the day. Boredom always made me smoke more. Sometimes, I would count the minutes a cigarette would last. It was supposed to be seven.

The sun was fading fast, and I knew the film would be wrapping shortly because I didn't notice any major equipment for a night setup.

I took my cap off to wipe the sweat from my forehead when I heard the welcome shout of, "That's a wrap!" The boring shoot was over.

When Williams returned, I informed him, "Since it's early, they'll either reassign us or allow us lost time (time accrued) to go home."

"Man, this shit was boring...I just wanna' split."

"You ain't kiddin'," I said. "Imagine if you were here alone. You'd be talkin' to yourself."

"I know, I know," Williams laughed. "They say anything about any features?"

"Not a word. I'll go and call for our assignments."

It was just before dusk when I called for the assignments.

Roll call Officer Spinell informed me there were no more jobs for the day, so we could go home or just hang around until the student film completely emptied the street of equipment trucks.

Next, he made a statement that floored me, yet he was unaware of how it profoundly affected me.

"Yeah, there's only Godfather III shooting interiors at the New York University Medical Center and they don't need anyone, so yeah, go home when you finish up."

I was stunned. My ass I'll go home! I thought.

I told Williams the score and explained we would be taking a chance going to a set we weren't assigned to.

"Hell, I wanna' meet Pacino," he replied.

So, remaining in our uniforms, we hopped in our cars and headed to the New York University Medical Center. I figured if we got caught, at least we we'd have our Pacino pictures. When we arrived, I immediately noticed the bright movie lights. Again, the crew would just assume we were assigned there, so I knew that would not be a problem.

Another plus was that there were no crowds. The location was on private property; however, the campers were not, so we had to hope no one approached us with a problem that maybe some nut was causing trouble hanging around the trailers.

The scene Coppola was filming was Al Pacino being wheeled in on a gurney, in character as Michael Corleone, who had just suffered a diabetic attack. Williams and I waited patiently for the scene to wrap.

"I can't wait to get a picture with Al Pacino!" Williams enthused. He was as excited as I was.

Then, there he was, Al Pacino, himself, walking to his camper in our direction! Nervously, and trying to be inconspicuous, we got our cameras ready. A bodyguard named Lou accompanied Pacino as they approached. Lou turned out to be a friendly ex-cop who had no problems with us. And I thought I had the dream job.

Pacino was in costume and makeup. Dressed as the aging Don, he appeared older than he was and somewhat frail. For some reason, he had also put on sunglasses, although it was night. But, hey, he was a movie star of the highest order. Ecstatic, we took pictures with Don Corleone, shook the Godfather's hand, and thanked him profusely.

Officer Williams was glad I'd talked him into going over to the hospital. For me, the moment was like when you meet a girl for the first time and she gives you her phone number. It's a natural high, like what Ganza described when he met Clapton. Meeting my favorite actor was no small thing. I had seen all of Pacino's movies and really believed he was the finest actor out there.

Ever since I joined the Movie Unit, I had been looking for Al. Now, if I wanted to, I could brag that I finally met the actor. I was elated on the drive home. Ever since I was a kid, I was a fan of Mr. Pacino. I would wonder what kind of girls he went out with, what he drank, and what kind of cigarettes he smoked. I even tried to dress like he did.

I hit a humongous pothole on the way home and, because my car was small, I felt as though the impact had lifted my rear end in the air. My car was also brand new; ordinarily; I would have immediately obsessed about my faulty driving. I would have been frantic that I might have done damage to the undercarriage. Uncharacteristically, though, I was not alarmed. That's how high I was. It was fitting that I had bounced up off the seat.

***

The following workday was slow, and the office had canceled my initial assignment. I decided I didn't want to take another vacation day, so roll call reached and found an assignment for me.

I was told to report to 90th street uptown to a private prep school where a production was shooting inside the building.

Spinell said, "Hey, pal, just hang around; maybe help the crew park a truck."

I was getting sick of his "Hey, pal" comments.

"Sure," I said.

When I arrived, the street was already lined with equipment trucks, production vehicles, and campers. The crew was working unusually quietly in the early hour, setting up tables and laying cable. When I asked what movie it was, I could not believe my luck.

The Godfather, Part III was shooting a funeral scene inside the library of the school, which had been made up to look like a parlor in an Italian countryside villa. By now, I realized that many film producers had the habit of sneaking back into town when the production was supposed to be finished. They would be re-filming scenes or extra shots that the director thought would be needed.

It appeared that I had arrived before any of the actors; however, I recognized Lou, Pacino's exclusive bodyguard. After we talked a bit, Lou asked me if I wanted some 8 x 10 signed photos of Pacino, and I was very happy to accept them.

Later, I would learn that Pacino also employed a regular driver (another dream gig that I would like to have) who chauffeured him around in an SUV with Al sitting in front. However, on this particular morning, Pacino showed up at work in a cab. Either way, remember, the Teamsters get compensated for the ride.

Pacino exited the vehicle, and Lou moved to his side. Al was wearing what was probably casual Italian, a loose-fitting, cool, light-beige number; it easily could have passed for Middle Eastern garb. His hair was full and back to a youthful dark color. I should have asked for another photo, but I didn't. Another regret.

The picture I had taken the night before was of Mr. Pacino dressed in character and looking old. With the magic of movie makeup, his hair looked gray and thinning, and he was wearing the dark glasses. It turned out not to be such a great photo in comparison to what could have been. But, by now, we know my quirks. I knew I would run with that thought for a long time.

Pacino walks with his shoulders hunched and his head down, so you really have to get up in his face to grab his attention. I decided that morning to leave him alone. I did not want to ruin the image I would have of him if he had said "no." Pacino also does not smile much. I had been told that by a couple of the cops who already had pictures with him going back a decade.

"If you don't get him just right, he doesn't smile," they said.

Many celebrities are, indeed, self-centered. I didn't think Pacino fell into that category.

I do have one buddy, Officer Torino, who possesses the ultimate Al Pacino photograph, and, for this reason I will mark Pacino down as a "photo failure" for myself. Torino's excellent shot shows him with Al on the Brooklyn side of the bridge with the Twin Towers in the background. There is a smile on the actor's face, and Torino's grin is also pretty apparent. Torino possesses a slight resemblance to the actor, with similar angular features and prominent (not big) Italian nose. However, Torino is a bit taller than Pacino, and he has slightly less hair, so, naturally, we busted his chops about that.

To top it off, the picture was taken during the filming of Scent of a Woman, the film for which Al Pacino won an Academy Award. This photo is so good that I consider mine a failure. It was another miss that would haunt me for a very long time. I would have used a similar picture for the cover of this book.

Back on 90th Street, just seconds after Al exited the cab, he suddenly looked confused, and then he took off sprinting down the street as if he were running for his life. Lou looked at me, befuddled, then took off after him.

What the heck happened? I was thinking he had left something in the cab.

Well, as it turned out, Pacino evidently promised the cab driver an autograph and forgot to give it to him. Not to disappoint a fan, he chased the cab to the next stoplight to offer his scribe. How cool was that?

Pacino made quiet, unnoticed gestures that made him all the more human, in my eyes anyway. During the filming at the hospital, production was informed of an elderly sick woman housed on one of the upper wards. She was a huge fan of Pacino and had been swooning at the idea of the actor being in the building just below. When Pacino was told about her, he went up to her room and gave the woman the surprise of her life. The woman was thrilled when she had her picture taken with the star. Pacino then signed an autograph for her and, more importantly, sincerely asked after her health. He made her dream come true. Now, that's class!

Richard Bright is a character actor who played Michael Corleone's bodyguard in all three films. Character actors were all part of the scene, and we took many pictures with them especially since access to these actors was easier. Mr. Bright kind of paused for a second to think about it when I asked him for a photo, although I don't know why. Anyway, click!

Talia Shire, real-life sister of Francis Coppola, and on-screen sister to Al Pacino, was no problem. As she was walking to her camper, I grabbed her. Well, not literally! She was singing an opera song when I approached. She put her arm around me for the picture, and the result is that she appears to still be singing.

Francis Coppola's daughter, Sofia, was playing Michael Corleone's daughter in the film, so this movie was all in the family.

***

That week, my strange luck continued, perhaps because exterior shooting had slowed. I was assigned one morning to the Silvercup Studios in Astoria, New York. Silvercup was an old bread factory, and it was located right beneath the 59th Street Bridge, on the Queens side. I was once again overjoyed because, for me, it was just a show-up assignment that actually turned out to be a pretty good picture day.

Although I had grabbed a fair number of pictures on The Godfather, Part III, I was still captivated enough by the filming to want to spend even more time on the set. I could never get tired of it. This was probably the final revision on the film, and my last chance to be around the Godfather family.

I had never been to the Silvercup and, walking around the set, I wondered what it must have been like on the old sound stages of a Hollywood back lot.

The Godfather, Part III set was dressed up for the big opera scene. There was a stage and a huge mural background depicting a small Italian village somewhere on a Sicilian hillside. The painting and its colors were meticulous and to the director's liking. This was the setting for the movie's finale in which Michael's son, Anthony, makes his opera debut in Italy.

On a nearby table, photo layouts of the stars in costume and various scenery shots were spread out. Truth be told, for a brief moment, I felt like helping myself to the unguarded photos, but, of course, I did not. I could only imagine the embarrassment of being caught swiping pictures, especially while in uniform, not to mention the trouble I would encounter with the Police Department.

This was my final chance for photos on a morning when there were still players working. I waited eagerly in the studio lobby for their arrival, all the time pacing back and forth like a kid at a ballgame waiting for his favorite players to enter the park.

For me, there was a real curiosity about the studio, hidden as it was in the industrial section of Queens, New York, of all places. I decided to walk around the first floor where there were some open dressing room doors. The rooms were clean and neat, but not glamorous nor even slightly fancy. There were no big stars plastered on the front doors, either.

All the rooms were empty except one. At a small, nondescript desk, Francis Coppola sat with his back to the door. He didn't notice me; apparently, he was transfixed by his portable processor and was lost in his Godfather world. He was typing rapidly — at least it seemed to be rapid to me, as I am a very slow and sloppy typist.

I envied the tenacity Coppola devoted to his work. Supposedly, he was writing and rewriting the day's draft, something he did throughout the entire course of the film. What he was reviewing were re-shoots planned for today, and he was still pondering fresh ideas, just in case.

I went outside to smoke a cigarette when, lo and behold, Al Pacino walked right toward me from where the campers were parked down the block. Celebrities were not required to use the dressing rooms; they were still entitled to their own trailers. As usual, his bodyguard was at his side, but then I noticed to his right was Andy Garcia.

I asked the bodyguard if he would snap a picture for me. Al was out of makeup and character, there were no crowds around to make him nervous, and it was the perfect time. However, Lou informed me it was not a good time, because the two actors were going over a scene they were to film. I lied and begged, saying that this would be my last opportunity for a photo because I didn't know how much longer I would be in the Movie Unit (how prophetic that lie was!).

Well, Lou was certainly correct about the timing. In the shot, I am smiling like the cat that finally caught the canary. However, Pacino isn't even glancing toward the camera. Instead, it appears that he is still in conversation with Garcia, gesturing with his hands to make a point. Regrettably, it was another missed opportunity for a great shot. I just couldn't get it right!

Later, inside the studio, I caught up with the great actor, Eli Wallach. He was such a gentleman, even insisting that he remove his glasses so it would be a better picture. Indeed, it was a fine shot with Mr. Wallach dressed in a tuxedo for the opera scene in the film. Soon after, I encountered the director's daughter, Sofia Coppola. She walked on the soundstage with her hair up in large curlers. Actors and actresses are constantly spiffed up between takes. That's why they are so captivating on screen. I've even seen a few stars whose teeth are not exactly as white as they are on the big screen. I asked Sophia for a photo.

"Look at my hair!" she said.

I told her it didn't matter.

"You look good," I said. "I really mean it."

Sofia was actually prettier in person than on film. I guess, for her, it must have been hard to live up to the expectations, especially with all the big-name actresses who were mentioned before she took on the role of Mary Corleone.

Scene XVI

A couple of days after the Silvercup assignment, I was shifted downtown to near the Supreme Court building. Peter Bogdanovitch was directing a light comedy starring Richard Pryor and Vanessa Williams. Both actors were receptive to photos with us.

As bowled over as we were with Vanessa's beauty, we were equally taken by the deteriorating condition of Richard Pryor. He could hardly walk and had to be helped to step up the lowest of curbs. Unfortunately, we heard that Mr. Pryor would not sign autographs for precinct cops that day. I understood; he appeared as if he barely had the energy to take a picture with us. I could not help but recall one of his flamboyant concerts in which he was full of vibrancy, vulgarity, and hysterics.

The Supreme Court building is a favorite for film studios because of its grand presence and flowing stairway leading into the building. It is also the court where young John Kennedy, Jr., was assigned during his stint as a new assistant district attorney. Kennedy was a fitness aficionado and usually peddled his bike to work. Actually, because of his love for fitness, he would be spotted by many New Yorkers around town, whether he was on his bicycle or throwing a football or Frisbee around on the lawns of Central Park.

One afternoon, I was driving north on Greenwich Street, and I spotted Kennedy cycling southbound past me. He had his pant leg rolled up away from the chain to avoid damaging his proper dark suit.

The morning of the Bogdanovitch shoot, John Kennedy happened to cruise right by us, stopping to dismount from his bike on the right side of the Courthouse.

Once again, I was with Officer Ganza, who was pretty adept at securing a photo. We made our way over to the Prince of Camelot. It was very early, and we were not yet dressed in full uniform, only in our police pants, and that would not make us recognizable as cops. Naturally, Kennedy didn't know who we were when we surprised him. Certainly, I could not blame him for his initial nervousness. Since he was a kid, I'm sure that thoughts of becoming the victim of abduction was never far from his mind. God knows what he must have endured all those years being constantly stalked and hounded by reporters and paparazzi.

We put John-John at ease immediately by showing him our shields and explaining who we were and why we were there. He was very nice about taking a picture with us and, for someone who was probably one of the most famous people in the world, he flashed no ego. The cops in the unit who had met Kennedy all agreed that he seemed to be a humble guy with no pretensions. He rarely had bodyguards and flashy automobiles. Frequently, he appeared to travel alone, just wanting to fit in with the city he loved.

I was terribly upset when he was killed in a tragic plane crash years later. My mom bought into the whole Camelot thing; when I was growing up, there was great admiration for the slain President and his family. The last photos of John Kennedy, Jr., showed a content man, often walking with his wife and their dog.

The picture Officer Ganza and I took was a good one, though hurried, because John said he didn't want to be late for work.

"I have to get in," he told us.

And, as he walked away, he turned back and asked, "Are you guys really cops?"

We laughed.

By now, the reader is familiar with my terms. The words "we" and "us" refer to the cops of the Movie Unit, or sometimes just any cops.

Those two words were never more apparent, as I gradually

found myself growing apart from my childhood friends and socializing more with cops with whom I had worked over the years. I was also spending more time with Christine and our families. Life goes in cycles, I suppose. But, in the meantime, I was still consumed with my like/dislike relationship with the Movie Unit.

Sometimes, when filming slowed, the rumor would circulate that our Unit was going to be disbanded to meet the essential needs of the Department. The higher-ups were contemplating using Borough Task Force cops and Precinct Units to cover the movies when, and if, it became busier.

Thankfully, as often happens with many rumors, this turned out not to be true. Still, every time the word was spread, the cops assigned to the Movie Unit would worry. Celebrity obsession aside, most of the cops loved the Unit and did not want to return to any precinct. They were on the "tit," as it was called, when lucky enough to be away from patrol duty.

There was no way any of them wanted to go back to the real world of policing and, for the moment, neither did I. So the Department's concession to the Movie Unit remaining intact was simple. If movie making slowed dramatically, they would whore us out to various precincts and add to the city's increased attacks on parking violations.

Now, instead of being assigned to most interior shooting, we would become glorified meter maids. We had no choice but to be taken advantage of.

Around this time, I got it into my head that I wanted to return to school. I thought I would take some writing classes and maybe some philosophy courses in the coming fall. Together, the subjects might legitimize my hobby. The Department, along with some city colleges, was offering discounted tuitions and flexible class schedules to accommodate the needs of police officers. However, my thoughts were stuck with procrastination...and...and....

***

Christopher Walken and Maria Conchita Alonso stimulated the Movie Unit's return to business when they began filming an action movie down by the South Street Seaport. The Seaport was always a great location where one could walk around and enjoy the scenery of New York's harbor. The Seaport, with its shops, restaurants, and views, created a New England stillness and an untroubled feel to the city.

Both actors were willing and affable, although, at first glance, Walken possessed the same intense look he displays on screen. This was the second time I had seen Mr. Walken in person. Not long before, I was working in Central Park when the actor jogged by one morning. He nodded to me as he passed, all the while keeping that intense look on his face.

***

I took a brief vacation to the Sunshine State in September and returned on a windy fall day. It was especially gusty down in lower Manhattan by Wall Street. I was assigned to work at a filming, but I had no clue what the movie might be about. My first day back on the job didn't exactly overwhelm me with excitement. However, the movie starred Danny DeVito, who posed with me for a picture in which he hammed up the shot with mock seriousness. It is one of the few pictures I have in which I'm noticeably taller than the actor standing next to me.

In Hollywood, it is fact that some of the shortest men are the biggest stars. I first saw the diminutive DeVito years ago when I was living in Los Angeles. It was one of those fine moments we cherish in memory. My uncle had landed me an interview with casting director Bobby Hoffman, who was known for his work on the television hits Happy Days and Laverne and Shirley.

From the window on the bus, I could see the huge scripted

word, Paramount, at the entrance to the studio. After stepping off the bus, I walked through the gate of Paramount Studios. What a big deal that was for me — my name was on a list at the front security desk of this famous studio! Suddenly, I heard a car pull up, and I turned to see Danny DeVito driving a small sports coupe. He noticed me staring at him, so he smiled and made a funny face. That's when he was in Taxi.

The part I interviewed for that day was a new sitcom Paramount was tossing around. The role was to be a friend of Scott Baio's character. Sitting across from this frumpy, casting guy who was dressed in a hideous leisure jacket and funny hat, I felt confident and thought I had a good shot at landing the role. How naive I was!

I didn't get the part, but it was thrilling to be there, nevertheless, scanning the images of Hollywood's dream factory, a world of make believe, sound stages, and production offices. That all took place in another time when dreams seemed possible, when my uncle bargained with me.

"Come to California," and "Come to Hollywood," and "Give it a shot!" he said many times.

Now, this was my Hollywood.

There were still days when I would receive an assignment and not know what the production was. Depending on who was answering the office phone, I wouldn't even ask.

***

It was early morning when I was assigned to a movie set that I thought was a low-budget affair. When I arrived, I was told the name of the film, Regarding Henry, but it didn't ring a bell. I was informed that the movie starred Harrison Ford and the up-and-coming actress, Annette Bening. Of course, I was eager to meet both of them. Ms. Bening was absolutely gorgeous in her role as a grifter in the movie, The Grifters. Annette Bening would soon become one of the finest actresses in Hollywood. Unfortunately, Bening was not on set that day, but Harrison Ford was.

This man's man was walking toward me on the way to his camper, pretty much unexposed; he was blocked from the public view by the line of trailers. Quickly, I grabbed a teamster and had him take the photo (getting better, aren't I?). Mr. Ford was very kind, as was the film's director, Mike Nichols. Harrison Ford is one of Hollywood's all-time major players. *My scorecard was growing!*

Scene XVII

Beginning its run in New York was The Super, a tailor-made, starring role for Joe Pesci. This was supposed to be his reward for his brilliant turn in GoodFellas. Rumor had it that Pesci was getting $900,000 for the movie, just shy of the magic million he would eventually earn.

The movie also starred Madolyn Smith Osborne and Vincent Gardenia. When I met the stout, hard-talking Mr. Pesci, I told him I thought he was crazy in GoodFellas. I'm sure he'd heard that a million times before. I'm also sure that his goal was to be just that crazy. Crazy enough to take home the Oscar.

Vincent Gardenia was an old timer whose credits were in a long line of films. His rough features and bear-down eyes, along with that distinctly pitched gruff voice, made him a very recognizable character actor in Hollywood. He was most famous for playing the Bunkers' neighbor in All in the Family, and for starring opposite Charles Bronson in Death Wish. Gardenia was also a native Brooklynite who never moved from his beloved Borough. When I met the actor, I mentioned to him that we had been introduced in a Brooklyn restaurant a few years earlier and that my dad had been the maitre d' there at the time.

I reminded Mr. Gardenia of the restaurant's menu special, "à la Gardenia." He laughed, remembering both the dish and my father.

Late fall took on the chill of winter and, on some days during the shooting of The Super, it was absolutely freezing, but the pictures were worth it.

***

Brooklyn was second only to Manhattan for favorite shooting locations, especially the Coney Island Boardwalk. There is so much history there. Just panning back from the Boardwalk to the old amusement park could conjure up a feeling of nostalgia, even for those who had never been there before. One could stand on the splintered boardwalk, look at the amusement park, and almost see the ghosts of the past. Vicariously, one could smell the delicious aroma of hot dogs, burgers, and other greasy delights; and the ears could almost hear the coaster screams and ghostly laughter, the screeching seagulls, and the thundering ocean waves.

Seagulls were especially bothersome in the summer, both with their piercing cries and their attempts to swoop down on food, even being so bold as to snatch morsels on the fly from children's fingers. Along the beach, muffled, nondescript conversations permeated the air.

But, when it's winter with the wind whipping around the boardwalk, Coney Island is a brutal and desolate place to be.

A made-for-TV pilot was being filmed on the beach close to the water, adjacent to the Boardwalk's extended and weather-worn pier. It was, hold on to your hats, a show about New York City Police Officers assigned to the Mounted Unit.

The pilot never took off, luckily for the potential star who would go on to star in another police drama, NYPD Blue. Dennis Franz looked like a cop; dressed in a mounted uniform, he was burly without definition, thin-haired, and mustached. We took a picture, and it came out great. I wished him luck and, soon afterwards, the role of Andy Sipowitz would earn the actor fame and a few Emmys.

A footnote to the above: I and my fellow officers in the Movie Unit could not stop ourselves from pointing out technical flaws in police-related shows. They were little things that a civilian would never spot. For example, there were uniform discrepancies, such as patrolmen wearing out-of-date uniform shirts or jackets; or TV sergeants would be wearing patrolmen's shields and vice versa. There was some seriously unrealistic Dragnet type dialogue, too.

***

Soon, there was a quick succession of photos logged in the bank. There were funnymen Eric Idle and Robert Wuhl filming — what else? — a comedy in Midtown. Then, I was surprised on a low-budget set when the star was F. Murray Abraham. The actor put his arm around me in a friendly gesture as we walked halfway up the block to the craft service table.

"How are you, Officer? Has everything been alright with the police?"

He was a real gentleman who admired the police, and he was an Academy Award winner.

Bob Uecker, of baseball fame, was doing his thing on the set of his famous Miller Lite Beer commercial that was filming in Central Park. He was shooting an exhaustive rollerblading scene going in and around small orange cones. I grabbed him for a photo.

***

Like many kids my age, I had been a huge fan of The Munsters when I was younger. Who could forget 1313 Mockingbird Lane? So, when I met Herman Munster, himself, it was with childlike pleasure. Fred Gwynne was an easy ask and a giant of a man.

"Hi ya, hi ya, hi ya!" he enthusiastically called out to me.

Gwynne then joked and told me that he didn't take a part in the recent remake of Car 54, Where Are You? because of the lousy script. When I met him, he was in costume filming the Woody Allen movie, Shadows and Fog.

Also on that film were actors John Malkovich and John Cusack. I took a picture with them when they made their way to the craft service table for a snack. Judging from the outside looking in, I thought the film had potential with its early gaslight, turn-of-the-century theme, its mysteriously murky black-and-white cinematography, and its cast of really fine actors.

However, it was not a good film and bombed badly at the box office. That's the mystery; even the best directors and actors do not really know how their movie will be accepted.

The days passed, and another chill moved in; it appeared that it would stay for a while. The workload slowed and, once again, the rumors abounded about the demise of our Movie Unit. Personally, it just didn't worry me anymore. I was growing restless working the cold streets on low budget commercials and student films.

The Super was still shooting scenes in a dilapidated building on the Lower East Side, but that assignment was tiresome. It was the same location, and I was standing outside on the frigid sidewalk. I suppose the thought had been festering, but this was a time when I seriously began to ponder just chucking it all and getting away from the cold and boredom. I had accumulated some nice pictures along with good memories of working on film sets. Maybe, years down the road after retirement, I could snag a job working as an actor or a technical advisor. Why not? Many cops did.

My first photo with actor and retired cop, Dennis Farina

Jack Lemmon, a Hollywood legend and one nice man

The beautiful Vanessa Williams

The worried Michael J. Fox

"I remember you." Danny DeVito

Stretching and wearing a hat, not event close to Tom Selleck

Sad Sack "Don Corleone" Al Pacino

The "Bohemian" Andy Garcia

"Gentleman" Joe Mantegna

The intense Christopher Walken

One of Hollywood's biggest movie stars, Harrison Ford

"This will be a good one." Robin Williams and Jeff Bridges

The consummate director, Francis Coppola

Bruce Willis surprised me with a handshake

The mellow guitar god, Eric Clapton

Ah, memories, Mr. Herman Munster, Fred Gwynne

"No make-up, no problem." Lovely Melanie Griffith

"Don't ask him for a picture." Martin Scorsese

"I want to be a rock star too!" Jon Bon Jovi

The super-gorgeous Halle Berry

Denzel Washington as Malcolm X, amazing!

Sweetheart, "Kay Corleone" Diane Keaton

Gorgeous Cindy Crawford left me speechless

"Vegas anyone?" Sarah Jessica Parker and Nick Cage

My uncle's pal, Danny Aiello

"We have to get a picture with Michelle." (Pfeiffer)

Breathtaking even in a t-shirt, sexy Sharon Stone

Christine, me, and Macaulay Culkin at Planet Hollywood

"You elbowing me!" Robert De Niro

My favorite TV Grandpa, Al Lewis

Supermodel heaven!

Last photo, music legend, Kris Kristofferson

Scene XVIII

Fall dragged into winter, and the opportunities for pictures decreased. In that time, I met Elizabeth McGovern, who was observing the filming of a ghetto-gang-type movie way uptown. Downtown, Billy Crystal was touching up the New York sequences in City Slickers. It appears to be a great photo that I have with Billy Crystal; in the picture he's all smiles. However, the picture doesn't tell the whole story. When I approached him, he immediately contorted his face in an obvious sign of annoyance. It was really a grimace. Perhaps he smirked because he was about to jump in a cab.

Pictures with stars can be deceptive. A number of celebrities appear to be willing participants, while some do not seem to be all that accommodating. But the reverse can also go unnoticed. Comedians utilize the art of exaggerated gestures and contorted facial expressions. The same could be said of their ability to fake a smile.

The NYPD was experiencing a stretch of decent reviews with the New York press. The press was especially high on New York detectives and their master skills at gathering leads in major cases.

"Super Sleuths" is what they were dubbed.

The members of the Movie Unit just wanted to know when our next lead into a photo op would be.

The holidays passed with my mood in an upswing. Sure, I missed my family down in Florida, but I was comfortable enough with Christine's relatives to get me through. Besides, Florida was only two hours away, so if I felt a dire need for family, I could always hop on a plane.

And so, as my relationship with Christine blossomed over

the holidays, I thought I would contemplate the future and maybe purchase a house. One time, I found a small cape that I really liked, but they turned down my offer of $110,000. Would anyone ever conceive the possibility that such a price would be considered an unbelievable steal?

Yet, for some 27-odd years, I had resided in the same Queens neighborhood. It was a part of me, and moving wasn't going to be easy. I would obsess over my decision ad nauseam.

Scene XIX

Realizing it was not as good as the first two films, The Godfather, Part III went 0 for 7 at the 1991 Golden Globe Awards and, subsequently, suffered the same fate at the Oscars. That year also produced Dances with Wolves and GoodFellas. I saw Dances with Wolves in one of the last, old, majestic theaters in Rego Park, Queens, New York, and, at the time, I thought it was one of the best films I had seen in years. Speaking of old, majestic theaters, perhaps the most glorious movie house of all was the RKO Keiths in Flushing, Queens.

For me, The Godfather, Part III was still the ultimate experience taken from the Movie Unit. It was like a shadow that followed me.

Once, on a commercial, I was talking to a middle-aged Italian gentleman who showed me his hands, palms down, as if there were some magnificent quality to them.

I was like, what?

"They used my hands in The Godfather, Part III," he said. "I was Pacino's hands when he wrote the letter to his children in the opening scene."

The wannabe actor was genuinely proud of his claim to fame, and I'm sure he's told that story a million-and-one times.

I was always meeting those who wanted to be actors. Many times, we sat in rooms full of movie extras, and all they did was talk about the business and read casting periodicals.

One extra told me that he was Pacino's double in The Godfather, Part III. Not for any stunts, rather, he stood in for Al for the positioning of the character for camera angles by standing on pieces of tape for shot measurements. Some double this guy was! He had been a cop and given up his career for a dream that he would one day be a working actor. Hey, I really can't fault him for that, though, because he had the balls to go for it.

It makes one wonder about the limits of pampering that's lavished on the A-list actors.

You can just hear the agent moaning, "No way is my guy going to stand on a piece of tape for the period of time it takes the director to make up his mind. He has no time to show up for a body-part shot. Get someone else for that! "

Imagine all the movies with those stand-in hands and feet!

Who knows why I constantly changed course, but it was about this time that increasingly serious discontent set in. The life I had imagined in the Movie Unit, mingling with celebs, parties, and networking, was fading. I wanted to go home and return to the job I had signed up for. It was a paradox-pattern for me, like my L.A. experience or my attempt at community policing. My "boredom meter" began ticking at a faster rate, only this time I would have to try to honestly figure out what would be good for me. What would I miss? Who would care? And so on...

Trapped in another cold, dull winter, I began contemplating my exit strategy. Suddenly, my thoughts led me to the idea that I was, indeed, a cop, and maybe that was what I should try to be, not some security guard standing idly around each day waiting for the two seconds it takes to get a photo.

Once more, I was leaning heavily toward a return to patrol duties — getting assigned to a precinct that would offer a warm radio car, and perhaps a good working partner to converse with throughout the day. Still, I trudged on, unable to come to a firm decision about my future.

I tried to rely on the ambiance of New York City to get me through the day. I would treat my assignments as a tour through New York, a romance, walking along with the likes of Audrey Hepburn's Breakfast at Tiffany's character, Holly Golightly. After all, there were plenty of people to watch along the bustling sidewalks where shoppers and tourists moved in unison, as if on autopilot.

In Midtown, folks tend to maneuver like scuttling bugs in and out of the wonderful shops and buildings. On Broadway, they weaved and dodged traffic. In the Village, they strolled leisurely on the narrow streets that held a lifetime of centuries-old stories. Apartments were filled with well-dressed company and the intellectual chatter of liquored conversation. Yes, I was just going to stay in that dream state until things picked up.

I would indulge in the magic of horse-drawn carriages; I would luxuriate in the old-world-but-rich experience of standing in Gramercy Park; I would walk the quaint Bohemian streets of Greenwich Village; and I would marvel at the skyscrapers and the architecture of the endless building relics. New York, bright with snow and wonderful holiday decorations, would dazzle me.

Wow! Was I trying to convince myself to stay, or what?

I was thinking as if I were in la-la land, where everything was wonderful and humankind was all around us, and we could walk around with our heads stuck up our asses.

What about the real city, where criminals could victimize the innocent in the blink of an eye? Where filth lurked along and beneath the sidewalks. Where people were outright rude to each other. Where the traffic was unbearable during those snowy and well-lighted seasons of joy. Where every purchase either cost a fortune or was tantamount to a rip-off.

The days would roll on through winter, eventually leaving behind refrigerator-type weather as well as the war in the Gulf. Any war has frightening possibilities, but, thankfully, in the Persian Gulf, we were easily victorious. During that time, I finally moved to Long Island, though not into my own house. Instead, I rented a tiny apartment where I could be within a mile of Christine.

I missed my old apartment; it was larger, I could walk to the store, and there were many memories there, but I kept upbeat with the thought of my future. But still, I missed that apartment.

At work, we were still able to sneak in some interior shoots rather than be on summons patrol. The days were long, but we managed to duck a lot of the cold because we worked in pairs or threes.

A footnote to the above: Sometimes, when I'd be working interior sets, I would find entertainment, variety papers, or rag periodicals lying around on a chair or table or carelessly tossed aside by movie extras who were trying to make it in the business. In one of the papers, two auditions were listed, one for a small part playing James Dean for a community theater, and the other was a college project that needed two actors to audition for a scene involving Michael and Kay Corleone. Hmmmm! Who was I kidding?

On another day, I was skimming through an old May/June issue of the Patrolmen's Benevolent Association (PBA) monthly magazine that I had in my bag of gear. Spring 3100 was the name of the magazine. On the cover, there was a lovely photo of the Empire State Building lit up on a clear night and watching over New York like a beacon. Prophetically, to the right of the Empire State Building stood the majestic towers of the World Trade Center.

There wasn't much happening in the Movie Unit in the beginning of the New Year. We kept each other busy with cut-ups and conversations only a policeman could love. Officer 'Ski liked to grab extra mini-bags of chips and cereal boxes from the craft service table to bring home for snacks. He would have them in the baggy pockets of his duty jacket and, on more than one occasion, he would feel the smack from one of the guys crushing the goodies in his pocket.

Everyone was a target for laughs. We had a sergeant who had a penchant for pushing his weight around whenever he was in the mood. He was an older Italian guy from the Bronx who probably would have loved to be a gangster. His vocabulary was laced with curses and a succession of da, dem, dese, and dose. Also, his hands were always flailing about when he talked.

"Where are dose guys? Dere s'posed t'be in da vicinity of da set!"

However, the good sergeant forgot one thing: the police

officer's penchant for hysterical retribution. You see, this tough guy was also vain. He was bald and decided to get himself a hair weave. It wasn't a very realistic one. During that winter, the sergeant decided to add some of his own photos to the "Hollywood wall" in the office that is adorned with pictures of various cops and bosses in poses with celebrities.

He was so proud of himself—until he realized one day that his photos had a new look. Every picture he was in was "improved" with a patch of green grass taped to his head.

He became enraged. "I catch who's doin' dat shit, I'll make life mis'rable fer dem!"

So much for his new, handsome look.

I could also be taken by surprise by various one-on-one talks. I was actually surprised one afternoon by Capezzio's interest in the arts other than the movies. First, let me say that when I worked with Capezzio, my mindset was completely focused on celebrity. When we were together, stars could do no wrong as far as we were concerned. But, in the end, I knew it wouldn't be wise to emulate them or lavish too much praise on any celebrity.

So, Capezzio and I were bullshitting on a commercial shoot one afternoon, and a guy walked by us clutching his Bible. He was preaching the word of the Lord in a rather animated fashion, which meant that most of his rhetoric was spoken only to himself.

"I don't know why cops keep writing the same old tired shit about detectives," Capezzio said. "Just look around. Look at this guy. There are so many other stories to tell."

Deep, I thought.

Scene XX

Finally, the winter passed, giving way to spring and bright, sunny mornings. Officer Taylor and I were assigned to an Emilio Estevez shoot. While the crew was filming in The Plaza, we were across the street in the 59th Street Circle, where horse-drawn carriages pulled up like taxis.

We were shielded by production campers, so many civilians would not see us as we laughed and told each other stories. I was gazing up at The Plaza on this gorgeous day, and the classic structure was showing off its skyline opulence.

The inside of this majestic hotel is nothing short of sheer elegance; it is large and bright with marvelous chandeliers hovering above meticulous, plush carpets. The walls are lined with the best tapestries money can buy.

On the sidewalk by the horse-drawn carriages, a tuxedo-clad Emilio Estevez was returning to his trailer, and he had to pass Officer Taylor and me, which was a perfect opportunity. Officer Taylor stepped up to the actor and told him he had to have his picture because he already had shots with the star's father, Martin Sheen, and his brother, Charlie. This brought a smile from Estevez, and we had our photos.

Taylor was so nonchalant about his approach. He was a big strong cop, but his personality could be goofy at times.

There were a few Italians in our group, but he would always kid me, "Did Christine make lousy spaghetti last night, and you threw it against the wall?"

"Yeah, yeah, that's what happened," I replied each time.

That always drew laughs from the guys. One thing about cops, the repeated jokes never seem to get stale. As Taylor approached 40, we all busted his chops about getting old. Who knew that the big 40 would come just as fast for us?

Moments later, as we were standing there, the legendary actor, Richard Harris, walked by and stopped to ask us what all the campers were for. We told him it was an Emilio Estevez movie, but the name of the film slipped our minds.

Mr. Harris replied, " I know who he is."

We took the opportunity to get a couple of photos.

The result is a picture of Mr. Harris eyeing me as if to say, "Are you for real?"

For the next couple of hours, Officer Taylor and I languished on the sidewalk as the inevitable aroma of horseshit filled our nostrils. Gone was the romance of horse-drawn carriages as the realities of New York crept in with the odor.

***

Later that week, I was in lower Manhattan working on a low-budget film with 'Ski. Mariel Hemingway was dropped off early in the morning looking extremely tired, as if she had just rolled out of bed. Unfortunately, she did not emerge from her camper for the rest of our shift, thereby preventing us from getting a photo op.

There was another actress on set whom we recognized as the female lead from the cult movie The Warriors. 'Ski asked her for a photo.

"I don't do pictures," she said, flatly.

I wanted to say, "You certainly haven't, lately."

It was the first time I had witnessed 'Ski being turned down, but I didn't rush into hysterics, maybe because it wasn't a Dustin.

Also on set was Jerry Stiller. He was at the side of the craft service table looking for a snack. We picked from the same craft service table. He was such a nice guy, asking after us, and glad to take a photo.

Like a broken record, again there was talk of our unit's disbandment.

"The Job needs more cops on the street," is what we were told.

Like 18 more was going to make a difference. But the news about crime statistics always made "The Job" paranoid. Those statistics constantly fluctuated, sometimes in favor, sometimes not.

There were two separate shootings in a week, and I mean real, honest-to-God, gun shootings. One shooting involved a cop—the other, a Mafioso. Since we've already established that we live in a celebrity-obsessed society and mobsters are certainly celebrities—at least in New York—the bad-guy shooting captured the front pages, while the cop incident was somewhere on page five. Unbelievable! Shamefully, a cop had to be killed to warrant page one.

The news was depressing; still, I tried to remain interested in the gossip columns hoping the allure still worked for me.

Now, my take on "The Job" pulling our plug was, go ahead!

It would be the perfect excuse to send me packing without actually forcing me to make a decision. It was only about the pictures now. I still had the constant desire to snap away and get as many as I could.

I wavered back and forth on my complaint issues with the whole film process. Friends and family would tell me I was nuts to leave. Christine was more understanding.

"It's your career. Do what you want, don't listen to anyone else," she said.

I wanted to bring anyone I knew to a movie set just so they could witness the fact that not every day was filled with the kind of excitement people outside the Movie Unit may have thought it was. I mean, people thought I could just knock on a celebrity's door and begin conversation.

"Hi, what about a picture?"

I would be hard-pressed to imagine that anyone who was

enamored with celebrity would find a movie set boring.

I guess the other issue was trying to convince myself that, as a sworn police officer, I was beginning to feel a little uneasy about the fact that my friends from patrol were facing problems in the real world while I was dealing primarily with entertainers.

In 1991, some important things were going on in New York outside the movie industry. The city was still trying to mend fences from the remembered Tompkins Square riot caused by the infinite wisdom of bureaucrats who decided to evict the homeless from the park. This decision brought the civilian do-gooders out in force, many brandishing cameras in an attempt to catch the NYPD abusing their authority. In a way, they were a different kind of Coparazzi.

New York was also busy planning a ticker-tape parade celebration honoring the heroes of Operation Desert Storm. The victors would march up Wall Street with their leader, General Schwarzkopf.

There was also tough talk coming from legislators who were pushing the idea of bringing back the death penalty. And the winds would blow again with New York facing another unavoidable riot in Crown Heights, Brooklyn.

But, despite my police guilt, which was short-lived, I remained just a groupie in uniform and, along with my cohorts in the Movie Unit, I stood pat, waiting for productions to arrive in the coming weeks.

Scene XXI

FF35 was the filming permit number for Frankie and Johnny, starring Al Pacino and Michelle Pfeiffer. The film was hyped to be the next Pretty Woman. I was just glad that Pacino and Pfeiffer were in town. The movie's director was Garry Marshall, who also directed Pretty Woman. Frankie and Johnny was to be based on the stage play of the same name.

However, the film script differed from the original Broadway production. On the stage, the story focused on realism as portrayed through the pain of physically unattractive characters. Obviously that wouldn't be the case in the film.

My first day on Frankie and Johnny was an exciting one for me because this was a major motion picture with two highly visible players. Marshall was shooting a simple dialogue sequence between Pacino and Pfeiffer by the subway station entrance at Union Square Park. Word-of-mouth is a powerful tool, because the crowd soon began to swell, filling the sidewalk and spilling out into the street.

The gathering crowd meant that we in the unit had to go to work. We roped off and closed a portion of the lane on Broadway to accommodate the camera angle. Then we stood out in the street to expedite vehicular traffic traveling south on Broadway. This was easier said than done, since most motorists would rubberneck, curious to see what was going on.

The pedestrian crowd soon became too large for the current restrictions, and the milling people began to impede the slow-moving cars, so we had to step in and insist on additional boundary guidelines. More often than not, New Yorkers will abide by the law and graciously stand their ground, satisfied with simply pointing in child-like admiration at the filming stars. Yet, there are those who just can't help themselves.

Another problem soon arose when the paparazzi reared their hounding heads. Like bees to honey, they swarmed around the roped area and began inching their way past the perimeters. Their cameras were poised and hung around their necks like honor badges. We treated the paparazzi as we would any local news team that showed up at a crime scene. They were granted a few feet of grace just in front of the rope.

However, these shutterbugs were very persistent, and their reputations preceded them. They had to quickly collect the shots they came for to prove their worth, so it was essential for them to behave in an annoying and belligerent way.

Pacino and Pfeiffer were to begin their trek to the set from their trailers, which were parked on 17th Street and on the sidewalk to the park. They were situated purposely between the equipment trucks and the cars in order to be out of the public's view. Still, the actors were unprepared for the large crowd, so the director, Garry Marshall, asked us if we could escort them from the campers to the set.

Hell, yeah!

Now, earlier, one of our cops had asked Michelle Pfeiffer if he could take a picture with her, and the actress responded by asking the officer if he could wait until later. Generally, that is not a good sign.

After Mr. Marshall made his request, we took pictures with him and made it clear we wanted photos with Michelle, as well. After a couple of safe escorts to the set, the actress obliged. We did not even bother Pacino, whom everyone already had pictures with, anyway.

Actually, Al was walking in front of Michelle when we took her to task, and he joked, "Ah, they want pictures."

It was weird to catch him in a moment without a bodyguard and in a playful mood to boot.

As for as Pfeiffer, she was beautiful, even though she was dressed in a frumpy waitress uniform.

This was one of many times I should have gone for it and taken another shot at Pacino. He was not wearing the aged makeup of the Godfather, and he looked more like himself. I had been looking for Al for quite a long time, and now it appeared I would see him often, as Ganza had said.

Al was an anomaly. He would never say hello, although I don't think he was rude. I just believe he was into his own head most of the time. Some actors are constantly thinking out their character over and over in their minds. I realized that must be a hard thing to do.

I admired and worshiped him as the best actor alive, as far as I was concerned. Had I become an actor, I would have loved working with him. I would later respect him even more because, in my opinion, he never got involved with the unnecessary vitriol that many of the know-it-all blowhard actors espoused.

I still find it difficult to watch a movie that stars a celebrity whose name would become synonymous with controversial and philosophical know-it-all opinions and advice regarding world or government affairs. Instead, they should concentrate on their art. By contrast, Al was very private about his affiliations.

***

The following day, I took a page from Capezzio and brought a copy of LIFE to the set of Frankie and Johnny. On the magazine's cover was Al Pacino posed as Michael Corleone. I wanted to get the magazine autographed. We know that I'm not usually an autograph hound, but this was special to me.

Regrettably, because of my chronic case of the nerves in certain situations, I asked about it, instead of doing it. I approached Lou, Pacino's bodyguard.

"What would be a good time?" I asked.

Lou suggested that, since there were always people around, I should give it to him, and he would get it signed for me. I had no reason to doubt the ex-cop, especially since he had previously volunteered to get me signed photos. So, I naively agreed. In this instance, I later questioned why I did not ask Pacino myself, if for no other reason than to see Pacino's reaction at seeing the magazine, although the actor probably would have had no reaction at all. But it is important to witness the signature.

Officer Capezzio told me emphatically, "When it comes to autographs, trust no one. Make sure you see them sign it yourself!"

Even when a fellow officer reached into Swayze's camper to get us a few signatures, Capezzio would still reiterate his claim.

Later, I would convince myself that Pacino's signature had to be the real deal. I even compared the autograph to the others I had received. I thought they appeared very similar, even identical, though, of course it wasn't fool-proof. After all, I am no handwriting analyst. Many autographs are scribbled sloppily. At first, I thought Capezzio was exaggerating and was maybe even too paranoid, but a teamster friend told me something very interesting—something I probably would not have believed coming from a person I liked and knew fairly well.

This particular teamster had been John Travolta's driver when the actor was in New York filming Staying Alive. At the star's request, he got to hanging around the trailer to keep fans at bay. One day, a pack of fans waited eagerly outside the camper hoping to get a glimpse of Travolta and also his autograph. A publicist had imprudently promised these fans 8 x 10 photos of the star.

The publicist didn't care that these folks would stick around all day if they had to. So, it was left up to the teamster to get the still photos signed inside the camper, then bring them out to the fans. They were not going to see Travolta emerge from his trailer. Well, my teamster friend did just that; he brought out many copies of the actor's photo. They were signed, sealed, and delivered to a bunch of very happy movie fans.

The only problem? It was the teamster driver who did the signing on John Travolta's behalf. What really repulsed me about the whole incident was that the fans were sincere people who went away happy, cherishing their "true" phony autographs.

I was turned off by this deception, and with good reason. Usually, the teamsters were good people, often stepping in to take pictures for us and, many times, filling our days with interesting conversation. But to sign bogus autographs? Now, I began to doubt my own experiences with not-witnessed autographs.

Memorial Day was fast approaching, and it was a foregone conclusion that wonderful weather would finally be upon us. But, once again, I was feeling the Movie-TV Unit blues and wondered if I should seriously consider a change. One deciding factor was the traffic. Even though I received pay for travel, traffic at times was abysmal.

No matter what the climate, there was always roadwork on most of the major thoroughfares, especially the Brooklyn Queens Expressway.

I called Christine. "I just sat in traffic for two damn hours...." She had to be thinking, here we go again.

***

One day, I had just come off the Williamsburg Bridge after being on the Expressway where traffic was jammed to a crawl. Finally, I hit Houston Street heading west. Then, traffic was almost at a complete stand-still. As soon as I could, I headed west and proceeded to the handball courts on West Houston where final scenes for Frankie and Johnny were taking place. Before I reached 6th Avenue, I noticed one camper parked on the north side of Houston. It looked as if a small photo shoot was about to take place—maybe still shots.

Of course, I wondered who it might be. I had only a moment to try to figure out what was going on, because I was stopped at a light. Suddenly, I saw Cindy Crawford, who had just emerged from the small camper. I couldn't believe my eyes as I watched her run daintily across the street. I knew I would have time to backtrack, because it was apparent that they were at the beginning of the shoot.

Quickly, I arrived at the handball courts with the intention of grabbing my partner for the day and sneaking off to the still shoot. When I arrived at the courts, the principal actors were finishing up. Pacino and Pfeiffer had just completed the scene where their characters are playing handball. The street was somewhat crowded because many admiring folks were watching the actors film their scene.

Pacino hopped in his chauffeur-driven SUV, the car of his choice, and he sat up in front, naturally. He was wearing his Yankee cap with the bill pulled down over his forehead. I guess he was trying to be inconspicuous.

Garry Marshall stayed to film background shots of the court. But, at that moment, it didn't matter. I grabbed Officer Capezzio and Officer Ganza and told them about the Cindy Crawford still shoot.

"Well, let's go!" Capezzio sang out.

We jumped in my car and raced back up Houston Street. I was so glad to be with our resident photographer. The timing was great, because, right at that very moment, Ms. Crawford was crossing the street toward her camper, appearing perfectly cool and natural on a warm May day, even though she was wearing a heavy wool coat for the shoot.

Capezzio wasted no time. "Cindy, can we get a quick picture?"

"Sure," she said. "We can all get in the photo."

"Oh, no," Capezzio said, with a grin and animated hand gestures. "We have to get you alone."

It was Capezzio at his best, taking charge with no intimidation. So, Capezzio and Ganza took each other's pictures. They didn't want me blowing it.

"Your pictures come out like crap," Capezzio whispered to me.

When it was my turn, I was nervous as hell, although I didn't have to worry about my smile because it seemed never to have left my face. I was probably feeling hotter than Cindy felt in that gorgeous white coat.

Ms. Crawford got up close and put her arm around me. When I turned, it was all there—her beautiful face, her chestnut eyes, the famous mole, all right there, inches from my goofy smile!

"What precinct do you work in?" she asked, her voice smooth as silk.

I swear it was like a scene from a comedy. I could not get the words out, not to mention that I almost forgot where I worked.

Finally, I answered in a tiny, nervous voice, "Movie Unit."

I'm partial to blondes, but here I was, practically cheek-to-cheek with one of the world's most beautiful, sexy women, and I was praying that I didn't sweat or have bad breath.

We thanked her, and the guys could not stop laughing.

"You were like Ralph Kramden," Capezzio laughed. "Umna, umna, umna."

However, when all was said and done, it was one of the brightest moments in my career.

***

When Frankie and Johnny was finished filming, I was relieved. Most people I knew were fans of Pacino and Pfeiffer, and some wanted autographs. I would have loved to oblige, but it stressed me out just getting my own. I was happy to move on to other films; I mean, it wasn't like Pacino was sharing a cup of coffee with us every day. I had looked into Pacino's eyes many times but never received even a hello; maybe it was the method acting thing.

Frankie and Johnny had put greater-than-average demands on us because of the popularity of the two stars. For example, it got to the point where production always wanted ordinary people kept far away. Remember what I implied earlier about film people being nice only when they needed something? Well, one of the last scenes filmed for the movie was to be a shot of Michelle Pfeiffer standing in front of the Port Authority Bus Terminal on 42nd Street.

Before the crew could get to work, the star's assistant came over to say hello. This very rarely happened; something was up.

"Hey, how are you guys doing?" she asked, smiling.

"Not bad."

"Are you busy?" she inquired, politely.

And there we had it; the questions with reason for pretext.

"Ms. Pfeiffer and Garry Marshall would like to know if you could escort Michelle to the set. They think there are some shady characters hanging out by the depot."

We had no problem doing what was asked of us, although, technically, if there were no problems, we were not required to escort stars. They were supposed to have their own security on hand.

Pfeiffer was dressed in jeans and a sweater, and I thought about asking for another picture but I didn't. As it turned out, there were no deviants hanging around. It was obvious that the appearance and the reputation of the famed bus terminal had Ms. Pfeiffer worried.

Scene XXII

The film, Light Sleeper, was beginning its NY shooting schedule. The movie starred Willem Dafoe and Susan Sarandon. The story was about a confused drug dealer who was leaning toward the side of righteousness. Dafoe was very nice about taking a picture with us. He was hanging out with costar David Clennon when we asked him.

We overheard Clennon telling Dafoe that everyone should be wearing T-shirts that say, "Operation Technical Massacre, Impeach Bush," to protest the brief Desert Storm war.

Sarandon was another matter. When we saw her filming, some of us would not even ask her for a picture. She had a notorious reputation for being anti-everything. Even so, we did have a couple of guys in the unit who did not care about politics, because a photo is a photo.

***

On one occasion, I was just standing around an old New York brownstone, kind of lollygagging, when Paul Schrader, director of Light Sleeper, emerged and began to pace back and forth. Schrader is a deep-thinking screenwriter and director whose credits include Taxi Driver and American Gigolo. He was still pacing and smoking when I asked him for a photo.

"My pleasure," he said.

When Light Sleeper moved to interiors that day, I was shifted to a commercial in front of the ABC studios on Columbus Avenue. As

I waited for the commercial to begin filming, I took the down time to explore the floors of the news building. Our commercial had its craft service area situated in the foyer near the news crew and the anchors.

There is definitely something to the fame game. I watched ABC news anchors waiting on the food line; they included Roz Abrams, Sam Champion, and Bill Beutel. Once again, I realized that, no matter what the level of recognition—even if you are seen only on TV in just one state as a reporter—you are famous. There is always an aura of importance around famous people. There are also plenty of fake salutations to go around. A cop gets accustomed to false pleasantries and, with a keen eye, could spot a pretend salutation.

Back out on the street was the actor starring in the commercial about New York's famous Eyewitness News Van. He was a character actor often seen playing mob types in television and the movies. In this commercial, he was playing a hot dog vendor who notices as the van goes by his stand.

He was to turn and point with a backwards thumb, and say, "There goes that Eyewitness News Van again."

The whole commercial was 30 seconds long but, somehow, the crew managed to fill the whole day by shooting 59 takes. That's how many times I had to stand in traffic and back that van up from the stoplight. It's one commercial I will remember!

***

One nice afternoon, I was in Gramercy Park for a Law and Order scene. I always loved Gramercy Park; it just had that feel of old New York, with its glorious brownstones and apartments closely situated as if they were in the center of town. The well-kept street surrounded the park that was closed off to the public. Vines clung to buildings like the dressing of a painting.

It reminded me of something out of The Age of Innocence.

Paul Sorvino was the lead in Law and Order at this point, although they changed the cast a few times. I scored a picture with the jovial actor, who seemed to have taken a page from Talia Shire by remaining in the trance of an opera moment. Actually, Sorvino had a huge presence resembling that of an opera star, and he was singing a melody lightly. He asked my name when I requested a picture.

"Sure, Vinnie," he said

Afterwards, we moved to the courthouse where Broadway actors Tony Roberts and Tovah Feldshuh were doing a scene for the TV show. A ten-year-old photo Capezzio had taken of Feldshuh on another shoot had blown her away.

The day was still short, so we moved again to a low-budget film where one of the actors was the kid from television's Growing Pains. The youngster, Jeremy Miller, was as fascinated with cops as we were with celebs, asking the usual questions about police work with much enthusiasm. He wanted his picture taken of me carting him off in handcuffs.

***

I still found it humorous when I would pick up a newspaper and notice a shot of a celeb from a job I was working one of the previous days. A few of us were assigned outside one of the studio soundstages on the West Side while Light Sleeper filmed interiors. Dana Delaney stepped out of a trailer in a very short robe. Word was that she was about to film the nude scene in the movie opposite Willem Defoe.

It wasn't a rumor that she was very nervous and did not want anyone lingering on set unless they positively had to be there. Believe me, we were quite serious about how we could manage to sneak in, but the crew was very diligent about that not happening. I did not bother her for a photo (another failed opportunity) though I should have, because she was in the paper the next day. Those sneaky paparazzi. I didn't even notice them.

I was later moved to another shoot by the American Museum of Natural History, where I met up with 'Ski.

The wonderful Jessica Tandy had no problem with us taking

pictures.

'Ski reiterated Capezzio's claim, "I have no choice but to let you take this. Do not let your hand shake when you snap it!"

Then the actress signed an autograph for 'Ski. Tandy was so gracious and reserved that she could have been anyone's cultured grandmother — one to love, for sure. Actually, the autograph requested was on an 8 x 10 picture with Ms. Tandy, and Capezzio, who left no stone unturned, had 'Ski get the photo autographed for him. Obviously, Capezzio knew ahead of time what 'Ski's assignment was.

***

As full of complaints as I was, time was still flying. Soon, it was the middle of July, and I was on the corner of 65th Street and Broadway smoking another seven minutes off my life. Jami Gertz and Dylan McDermott were filming Jersey Girl. I never saw the actor, but I did get a picture with Ms. Gertz, who was standing on the top steps of her camper peering around as if someone might be watching her. Another actress happened by, the blonde soap star Tonja Walker, and she took a picture with me. Around Manhattan, soap actors often can be spotted, especially uptown where the soap studios were. Of course, they had more anonymity than movie actors.

I was good with faces. Not only could I spot major movie actors, but I could also pick out soap stars, sports stars, ex-mayors, some authors, and character actors, as well. There was always somebody notable walking the sidewalks of New York. That was the best part of people-watching in the Big Apple.

While I was still milling about on Broadway, an older woman approached me. She was petite, distinguished, and poised, wearing a brown shawl and matching fedora. She asked what was going on. Many people, of course, would ask that same annoying question. Curiously, though, this woman injected some talk about writing into the conversation.

She told me she had been writing for thirty years and was just recently feeling discouraged that her work had gone unrecognized. I felt terrible for her and, of course, for my future prospects. Another thing I supposed about writers is that many of us really don't want to be writers. The work is a seesaw of pleasure and pain, and the reality of recognition is extremely slim.

***

The following day, I was in Brooklyn, in the Brighton Beach section. An offbeat comedy club called Pips was shooting a promo tape. The skit was actually distasteful and complete with a warped sense of humor. The crew set up a mock motorcade and filmed a political satire of the JFK assassination, only this limo was complete with dummies resembling Laurel and Hardy and Jerry Lewis — all along for the ride in the ill-fated motorcade. I laughed at the silliness of it; however, when they exploded the likeness of JFK's head, I could not help but get an eerie feeling about the tragic events of 1963.

***

There was a different kind of simulation shoot that week; it was the Channel 2 News, New York, Shame On You segment. Shame On You was a popular part of the network's program because it often helped those who were swindled out of money and property, and those who had general, annoying complaints. They filmed in a small desolate alley in lower Manhattan, and anchor Arnold Diaz was dressed like Arnold Schwarzenegger, walking tall (not as tall as Schwarzenegger, though) through puffs of smoke blowing out from a small fog machine. He was promoting the spot, "Shame On You Will Terminate You."

Ironically, the residents above the alley were complaining about CBS and the late-night shoot, and the noise the crew was making.

***

Another day downtown, and I was assigned to another music video. Richie Sambora, of Bon Jovi, was filming a cut from his solo album. He was a nice guy who went out of his way to say hello and ask after the New York Police Department. Small things like that always meant a little extra to us police officers. The crew invited me to dine on Mexican food with them, and Sambora, rather than segregate himself, sat with the entire production.

Scene XXIII

Billy Bathgate was rolling into town, and I was thrilled because that meant another shot at Dustin Hoffman. But, like many previous assignments, I had to wait my turn on the food chain line. Instead, I was posted in Brighton Beach for yet another incoming Pacino film, Glengarry Glen Ross.

Again, the crowds came out for, "AAAAAAL," and they sang out his name with a long, drawn-out sound. I mean, this guy was in his fifties, and there were woman on rooftops in Brooklyn shouting down to him. Al was looking good, too, well-groomed, tan, and fit. He moved with poise rather than with the shuffling gait he used in The Godfather, Part III. He was wearing a sharp, designer Italian suit for his role as a shifty real estate salesman. Once again, we had to cordon off an area to tighten up the set. At least I was left on the right side of the rope.

Pacino's makeup girl was also looking good. It turns out she was Mrs. Rob Lowe. Glengarry Glen Ross then moved over to Brighton Beach, where I grabbed pictures with Jack Lemmon and Kevin Spacey, two brilliant actors who were both nicely accommodating. Mr. Lemmon, of course, was a movie legend. He could act rings around today's lime-lighted celebrities, yet he was such a nice guy and humble, as was Spacey.

***

Same week and now at a Midtown location, I got pictures with Ed Harris and Alan Arkin, who were both in the film as well.

It was a rainy day and, when asked for a photo, Ed Harris said, "I'd be glad to," while Alan Arkin's facial expression conveyed he was not thrilled with the idea.

However, for the deception of pictures, Arkin is smiling in the photo.

***

Summer was fading, and the riots that took place in Crown Heights, Brooklyn, which pitted blacks against Jews, raged on for three long days. It was not a good time to be a New York cop because, though "The Job" ordered multitudes of police to the scene of the riots, they once again restrained them from doing their jobs. The movie cops were not dragged into the melee. Instead, on one afternoon, Officer Sorkorski and I were downtown for a NY scene from the movie Honeymoon in Vegas. We scored pictures with Nicholas Cage and Sarah Jessica Parker. 'Ski wished them well on the movie, and Sarah joked that she hoped to have better luck since all her series had been cancelled. We walked close to the actress back to her camper, and 'Ski and I both agreed that Ms. Parker smelled delicious.

***

I stacked about a half-dozen more photos by summer's end. The movie, Used People, starred actresses Doris Roberts, Shirley MacLaine, and Kathy Bates. I got to meet only Ms. Roberts, who was very nice about the photo thing; she was like the friendly neighbor lady next door. Also in the movie was the great Italian actor, Marcello Mastroianni. He was standing against a wall dressed in a tailored suit, like an ad for a foreign film. He agreed for a picture with no problem, though I don't think he understood much English, since he just nodded.

***

I was still hoping to get another crack at Dustin Hoffman on the Billy Bathgate shoot. Knowing he was in town, and having the painful memory of my previous attempt, made the quest that much more significant. I wish I could have convinced the actor the first time that it would be a quick picture.

Filming continued on Billy Bathgate in Greenpoint, Brooklyn, first on a side street, then down by the piers. Talk about the atmosphere of a movie set! The crew had the whole block set up for the 1930s period. Rigged in the center of the street was one long dolly track. The mounted camera glided along, filming the extras as they walked on the sidewalk in period wardrobe.

Store fronts and street signs, along with the entrance to the subway, were all dressed up for the historical time of the movie. This was a magical way to film a movie.

Nicole Kidman appeared for a brief moment, but I hesitated and failed, once again, to get a photo of her. We know what happens to those who wait. She was magnificently tall and quite beautiful with a warm-greeting smile. I remember thinking how lucky Tom Cruise was. I did get a picture with Loren Dean, the young man who played Billy, and I also got a picture with the famed director, Robert Benton. Still, I was once again disappointed because Hoffman never surfaced, and so another failure thought ran through my head for days afterward.

***

The summer went out with a bang, literally. I got one of the other officers in my unit so pissed off that we nearly came to blows right in the street in front of a film crew. Officer Lanny and I were assigned to a college film class in Red Hook, Brooklyn. It was a very dull afternoon.

When our supervisor visited us, he let it be known that

Officer Capezzio and Officer Fontaine were only a mile away under the Brooklyn Bridge; they were assigned to a still shoot with some models.

When the boss left, I asked Officer Lanny if he'd mind if I shot over by the Bridge to see which models were there.

"No, go ahead," he replied.

I was thinking, why shouldn't I? Here I was on this shit video while two of my associates were getting paid to watch beautiful women strut down the cobblestone streets. I wasn't supposed to leave my set, but hey, at that point, I no longer cared as much as I used to.

Under the Bridge, there were a number of campers, and the crew was scuttling equipment up and down the street. There they were—Cindy Crawford, Stephanie Seymour, Tatjana Patitz, Linda Evangelista, and Naomi Campbell. I'd hit the Supermodel jackpot! Funny thing about the supermodels as opposed to other celebs—they were actually as gorgeous in the flesh as they were in their photos.

"These girls have some bodies!" Fontaine whispered.

The supermodels had bewitched us all. Capezzio helped me get my shots with all the models except Campbell, who was on a portable phone the whole time with Robert De Niro.

Cindy was, as usual, cool and sexy, wearing a dark blue sundress. She had just finished signing autographs for cops from the 84th Precinct. She signed the bulletproof vests they were wearing. I nervously mentioned to Ms. Crawford that I had once met her on Houston Street. No surprise that she didn't remember.

I never returned to my assignment back at the Red Hook projects, just assuming and expecting Officer Lanny to cover for me and sign me off, which he did. It turned out he was furious. The next time I saw him his eyes bulged, and he looked like he was about to spit venom.

We were teetering on the edge of a very bad situation—arms flailing and exchanging verbal blows that easily could have morphed into physical confrontation. It started rough.

"Get over here, I gotta' talk to you!"

When I heard that tone, I knew something was up, but I followed him away from the set.

"You're an asshole!" he shouted. "Where do you get your balls?"

Of course, I knew what he was talking about. Still, he took me by surprise. Capezzio and Torino could be hotheads, but Lanny was, well, kind of mild-mannered.

"You said you had no problem with it," I reminded him.

"That was before you screwed me. I had no idea it would be for the rest of the tour, you fuckin' moron!"

Now I was pissed. "You know what? Go fuck yourself, you asshole."

"No, you're the fuckin' asshole!" he shouted.

We were acting like two mutts in the street. Thankfully, we wound up walking away from each other as the teamsters and crew were obviously staring and commenting to one another.

One teamster actually asked me, "What the hell was that?"

But the teamsters, especially, could understand. They were nice guys, but they were street-smart and had had their own share of arguments with anyone who would make a smart-ass remark.

It really is a funny thing about people and their situational moods. If it had been Capezzio who drifted from Lanny, it would have caused the opposite effect. Lanny would even have gone as far as asking Capezzio if he got good pictures; that's how much he looked up to him.

It didn't matter much to me anyway, because, as it was, I had more important things to worry about. Christine had basically told me if I could not make a serious commitment, she would have to move on. Indeed, she had been extremely patient and careful with my feelings for a long while now. All the movies and dinners could go only so far. This girl deserved flowers and a ring. But I also thought she would cool her heels and step back to give it more time.

***

Soon after, on a September morning, we were once again on the move for summons duty, patrolling in Astoria. Since we were close to the Astoria Studios, we took a ride by. We saw Al Pacino walking up and down the block. Obviously, he was filming inside the building, but we couldn't figure out why he was strolling around. Another habit of the wandering method actor, I figured.

***

I called in for my assignment and was told it would be another commercial. I didn't want the commercial, because I was eager to find out what celebrity I would encounter next. That person would be my 100th photo!

"Ah, Vinnie," the roll call officer said. "Take good care of the trailer on that shoot, it's Michael Jordan's."

"Michael Jordan! The Michael Jordan?"

"That's the one, pal."

Something was wrong. It wasn't as if Jordan was in every day. I couldn't believe I was getting the assignment. What, was everybody else off today?

That night, I got a call from Capezzio. I never before received a call from Capezzio. Sure enough, he asked me to let him know what time the shoot would get under way. He must have been on vacation, or it would have been his assignment. Actually, I couldn't figure out why I would get the assignment to begin with.

I anticipated a large crowd the following morning when I arrived at the park and basketball court on Houston Street. After I'd been there a half-hour or so, and the park was still desolate—there were no orange cones and no sign of a film shoot—I called the office. As my luck would have it, the shoot had been cancelled; there would be no hoop star today.

I was then posted to Broadway and 174th Street, where a new

film was in town, The Pickle. Disappointed, I headed to the location where a crew was doing montage shots of the street.

Scene XXIV

Melanie Griffith became my 100th photo. She was so sweet and smelled good, too.

"I'll look better after makeup," she said.

I was totally satisfied with the way she looked right then, sweatshirt and all. I once saw her standing in front of the 83rd precinct taking photos with as many cops as could stream out of the place.

Ms. Griffith was starring in a new movie, A Stranger Among Us, and the great New York director, Sidney Lumet, was at the helm.

Mr. Lumet asked 'Ski and me if we could escort him around the Bellevue Hospital area to scout for some location shooting.

Hell, yeah!

We drove around the area near the famed hospital with the director in the car as if it were no big deal, which it was.

I informed the director that I had recently seen him on television doing an interview. Mr. Lumet laughed, and then responded in a reserved and intelligent manner, telling us he did not mind interviews.

"My best interview," he said, "was with Bob Costas. I couldn't believe it. Costas must have boned up on all my films overnight. He knew everything."

Too bad I couldn't interview Mr. Lumet, because I knew a lot about his films as well.

The director also confided in us how upset he was about the pending boycott from the New York production crews. The high costs of filming in the Big Apple were pissing off the movie studios. Lumet did agree that motion picture companies had the right to be fed up with the money demands from unions.

Many of the major companies were threatening to film in Canada, where it is remarkably cheaper to film movies. Actually, there are quite a few movies filmed in Canada, where the city landscapes pretend to be New York. A good eye for movies could spot that deception, though.

Ultimately, Lumet did film in Canada, which, for him was an unprecedented move. Like Woody Allen, Lumet had filmed 99% of his movies in New York, including Dog Day Afternoon and Serpico, starring — who else? Pacino.

I thought it was the ultimate pleasure to have Sidney Lumet in our car.

When he got out, he pushed his glasses up and thanked us, calling my partner and me by the wrong names, "Thanks Wally; thanks Bradley."

Mr. Lumet was photo #101, but I was still thinking about picture #100, because it would have made a good swan song to finish up with, as I was now more than serious about leaving the unit. I felt that one hundred photos were plenty, and that it was a good number to end the novelty.

By day's end, the wind was kicking up debris around the hospital, and some particles got in my eye. I washed my face and rubbed my eyes, more concerned I might miss the opportunity for more pictures. There lies the paradox and the drug of celebrity. As long as I was in the Movie Unit, I wanted more, despite my doubts.

Like Pacino, in The Godfather, Part III, I wanted out, but the lore kept pulling me back. The sharp contradiction was that, when I met people like Sidney Lumet, I did not want out. When I took pictures with actresses like Melanie Griffith, I did not want out. When I viewed New York through the camera, standing on the Brooklyn Promenade on a clear day with the New York skyline laid out before me like a perfect post card, I did not want to leave. When Manhattan was layered with a blanket of freshly fallen snow before the messy slush appeared, I didn't want to go.

My romantic side kept telling me that New York is really a gift to the world. Maybe it wasn't just a manufactured visage? My head was spinning again. I was lucky, wasn't I? I thought about the early days and the Penny Marshall incident when I was flippant about my duties. Thankfully, I never paid a price for that behavior back then.

When I let it leak that I wanted out, Officer Capezzio grabbed me at our next job together. "What, are you nuts? Don't get discouraged. If Pacino is approachable, anyone is."

And the actor was approachable. He was walking back to his camper with Michelle Pfeiffer, without his bodyguard and out of view from the crowds at Union Square. He appeared to be in a good mood, and the timing was perfect.

"They want pictures," he joked to Pfeiffer.

And we got our pictures with the actress, and I could have asked the actor again. But…

So Capezzio thought my disenchantment was about the pictures. That was more than partly true.

***

The day after the Lumet film, I was on the Coney Island Boardwalk assigned to The Pickle. It was sunny, but very windy. The annoying seagulls were chirping away endlessly and without harmony. I walked toward my friends to relieve them when I noticed the three of them laughing as they looked in my direction.

"OK, what now? No, I didn't eat a whole sleeve of Oreo cookies last night."

Recently, I had put on a few pounds, and I didn't help any by confessing to someone that I snacked late in the evening on cookies. In our world, if more than one person knows a secret, it becomes everyone's secret.

"Hey, hey, where's the Fonz, Chachi?"

What the heck were they talking about? I didn't get the joke.

"Get over here, Chachi," Officer Torino said. "We met your

uncle. He told us all about the part you tried out for in California."

There was more laughter, and this time I joined in.

"Hey, Chach, your uncle is great," 'Ski said, with the widest of grins.

Shit! My long-lost uncle from L.A., still trying to carve out a life in the movies, managed to get a gig working as Danny Aiello's assistant on The Pickle. The interview I had with casting director Bobby Hoffman, back in the 70s, had become a topic of conversation among my uncle and the cops in my unit.

Son of a gun let the cat out of the bag, I thought.

I wasn't prepared for it because I hadn't seen my uncle in years. I knew that he was acquainted with Aiello from his early years, but I didn't know he would be in town working with the film. In his defense, he didn't know the cop mentality of using one's personal information as fodder for ammunition. It was as if he had unleashed a verbal pit bull. I was the butt of jokes for weeks.

The Pickle continued its filming along the Boardwalk where I took pictures with Danny Aiello and Shelley Winters, who played his mom. Aiello was like Dennis Farina, a realistic Italian.

I reminded Danny Aiello of both my uncles, the one who was traveling with him, and the one whose restaurant he used to frequent back in the day.

"Holy shit!" the actor exclaimed. "Tre Amici. How is your uncle?"

It felt great that he recognized my family.

Shelley Winters was a trouper about taking pictures, even when she was exhausted. "Please hurry," she said. "I'm very tired."

She looked it. They filmed a simple scene where she and Aiello embrace for a mother- and-son moment, but it took hours. Shoot! At least, Ms. Winters made an attempt, even though it was a crappy movie. She could have just sequestered herself in old Hollywood, high in the hills of L.A.

***

Moving to The Plaza again, we were assigned to a spot where some celebrity was sure to walk by. One day the owner himself, Donald Trump, happened our way.

"Hi, guys," he said.

It was always easier when the celeb said hello first. Donald Trump is actually a New York kind of guy and is known to have great respect for the NYPD.

A few moments later, the boxer, Ray "Boom, Boom" Mancini got out of a taxi and we grabbed him, as well.

After Torino and I got our pictures, Officers Gorman and Calhoon showed up after being reassigned to The Pickle shoot.

Simultaneously, they hit me with laughter and, "Hey, Chachi!"

"You guys, too?" I groaned.

Working a number of days at The Plaza kept my pulse beating a little faster. Even when one is on the verge of boredom, the hotel is a unique place to be around. The Pickle set was closed off in the area around the cascading water fountain in front of the hotel. Police barriers surrounded the set, and the fountain blocked much of the view from the east.

If I stood a small distance from the flow of the pedestrian traffic on Fifth Avenue, I would avoid many of the observers and their stupid questions. What I tried to do most days was plant myself inside the filming arena.

I did manage to get a few more pictures on the set of The Pickle. The director, Paul Mazursky, was well known in Hollywood, so we bagged him. Isabella Rossellini, who was in curlers, was on set the same day as Ally Sheedy. I finally caught up with my uncle and got to chide him for a couple of days.

"Hey, Unc, you killed me with the Chachi thing." We both laughed; it was really harmless.

"See what you could have had?" he said. "You should have gave L.A. a shot back then. All those actresses you could have kissed doing scenes!"

What could I say except, "I know, I know. And I know that I'll never know...but, hey, this is close."

That's how I reacquainted myself with Uncle Joe. Boy, how I had missed him! He looked good too. Sure, he was older, but his white hair complimented his California tan. And he was still playing the part of agent, sporting a dark silk neck scarf, the kind tied by a small gold ring. Along the way, he had copped a few small acting roles playing tough guys. I was so happy to hear that. The years go by and, well....

One note on The Pickle: A lot of craziness happens in New York. There are car accidents and lousy weather conditions that sometimes rock and tip the trees, both real and fake. That said, a prop tree fell on my new car and dented the hood. Obviously, the fake tree was not held down tightly enough. That's my Pickle story and, believe me, that dent bothered me for quite a while!

***

I was set for another vacation, and I needed it. I needed to bond again with those I loved and escape from the fantasy. But, before I signed off for a couple of weeks, I managed a few more photo ops. Two of the subjects just happened to be walking by on the street. Bushy-haired comedian Eric Bogosian was just strolling along in Tribeca, and Kate Jackson, one of the Angels, was walking in lower Manhattan.

In Central Park, a Dutch comedy troupe was shooting a movie with its homegrown actress and very buxom blonde, Tatjana Simic. We took pictures with her and the entire cast, because we believed that the film was going to be a sleeper (a huge hit). It wasn't.

The fair and comely Mia Sara was in a Ridgewood, Queens, cemetery on the Sidney Lumet movie, when I asked her for a photo.

Former Mayor John Lindsay had just stepped off the red carpet entranceway to The Plaza, and I asked him for a photo. The police once called Lindsay "Boss." He took the picture with us, proud of his Finest. He was older, of course; but still possessed an air of dignity. Tall and erect, he was the shadow of a once-handsome man.

***

Fall in the city was especially beautiful in places like Central Park, where the foliage gathered en masse like a scene out of Thoreau's Walden. Tall, and with a calm demeanor, considering that he was a rock star, Don Henley, of the rock group the Eagles, was shooting a commercial in the park to plug his quest for the greater good and the ecology of Massachusetts's Walden Woods and its popular pond. The scene in the commercial had Henley walking on a narrow, hilly path crested by trees. He was speaking about the preservation of Walden Pond in all its glory.

The actual spot seen on TV does show flashes of Henley's pet project, Walden Woods. Then the commercial goes to dialogue where Henley's path to conversation is all Central Park. That's the brilliance of the camera's eye and the imagination of show biz. Don Henley was gracious, though, when I asked him for a picture.

***

There was one more photo to get before my vacation commenced. I was assigned to a low-budget film. It started with interior shots, but we were needed because they were supposed to go outdoors. 'Ski and I were sitting in the patrol car just kicking back, skimming the newspapers and shooting the breeze in front of the location, when someone knocked on the driver's side window. We snapped to, because at first we thought it was NYPD brass. We didn't want to appear to be dozing, which is cause for suspension. Also, when someone invades a cop's space by knocking on the window, our suspicious radar immediately goes up anyway. I rolled the window down.

"Hi Officers, I'm Harvey Keitel. If you guys need anything, let us know."

"Hey, Mr. Keitel, how's it going?" Ski asked.

"Good, good," the actor replied.

"Thanks for the offer, Mr. Keitel," I said.

We did need photos, and we got 'em!

The film Mr. Keitel was shooting was an independent movie called The Bad Lieutenant. It did not fare well in mainstream, but it was a good—yet provocative—film about a man's attempt at redemption. That's always a great theme. There were many vile scenes and crude dialogue in the film, but nothing that I hadn't heard on the NYPD, or even when I was growing up, for that matter.

Scene XXV

On October 15, President Bush was in Washington Park to dedicate the Law Enforcement Memorial to Police across the nation who gave their lives in the line of duty. It was the kind of ceremony that really appreciates the police and acknowledges the well-deserved attention that put a police officer's life in perspective. Seated behind the president, along with scores of others in the law enforcement field, was ex-cop-turned-actor, Dennis Farina.

In the same week, Senator Daniel Patrick Moynihan visited the 13th Precinct to show his support for the police. Before I was a policeman, I was a bartender at a Penn Station commuter bar. I had the privilege of serving the Senator and a friend a few glasses of wine. They left me fifty cents. Cab Calloway was also in one afternoon—three drinks—fifty cents.

Speaking of support for the police, I will note that not all are blind to our plight. Hollywood megastar Michael Douglas, playing a New York cop in Black Rain, was filming in New York when, one night, a real police officer was shot uptown. Strong word had it that Mr. Douglas called the hospital to inquire about the wounded officer's condition. The same thing happened when Harrison Ford was filming in NY. Another shot officer was in the hospital and Mr. Ford called to ask how he was.

Yankee owner George Steinbrenner sponsored what was called Silver Shield Day at Yankee stadium. Silver Shield Day was a ten-year program in which, once a year, a Yankee game was played to honor and help finance a non-profit organization through which the children of fallen New York City Police Officers and Firefighters would receive college educations.

The foundation had raised $1.6 million, and the Yankee slugger of the day, Kevin Maas, was all for it.

"I think it's great," he said. "A very positive event."

I returned from a peaceful Florida vacation, well rested and happy. I was able to spend some time with family. When I landed at JFK, a friend of mine met me at the baggage claim. Standing a few feet from us, waiting for his bag, was baseball great Willie Mays. Other than his famous face, one would not know it was Mays. He was plainly dressed in a velour sweater and tan polyester pants. It was nothing like the fashion statements worn by ballplayers now, not to mention the method of travel back then — flying coach.

With my friend Bobby leading the way, we walked up to Mr. Mays. One would assume that, by now, I had gained enough experience for a smooth approach.

However, before we even opened our mouths, Mays said to us rather sternly, "I'm not who you think I am."

Obviously, he did not want to be bothered, so we just walked away. Some others were not always that considerate. Their persistent, Capezzio-like attitude often paid off. Moments after we were rebuffed, we witnessed a passenger coax an autograph out of the slugger. For a second, I thought about Mickey Mantle's restaurant and how the place was always crowded. Certainly, Mays could have had his own joint.

Back in the police world, the Department was once again making its pitch for solo patrol cars. Of course this did not affect me at the moment, but it certainly might down the line. It was just a preposterous attempt by the city government to use as a weapon in a contract negotiation. The PBA insisted that such a policy could never be enforced.

"What works for small-town departments around the nation does not mean it will work in New York," the Union stated. "It is simply too dangerous for one police officer to handle assistance calls by him or herself."

Once again, the Movie Unit was preoccupied with the fall lineup. It did promise to be a busy season with five feature films on the calendar. Malcolm X was shooting in Harlem; in SoHo, it was Mr. Saturday Night, and Woody Allen's unnamed film (Woody's films were always unnamed).

The Distinguished Gentleman was filming by the South Street Seaport and, in planning, was the sequel to the popular Home Alone.

There would be plenty of overtime, which was another problem for me, because 12-to-16- hour days would cause me to fidget and smoke more. The guys hated my complaining about the overtime because, understandably, they loved the extra pay.

***

Director Spike Lee had his crew dress Lexington Avenue and 121st Street to look like Harlem in the 1960s. Store signs, automobiles, streetlights, and other props covered modern-day appearances and took the film back to another time. Period pictures were just wonderfully dressed up.

Visitors were popping up on the famed set. Mayor Dinkins was around, along with Al Sharpton and Mike Tyson, to name a few.

Denzel Washington was brilliant as the slain controversial civil rights leader. In fact, in the photo I have with the actor in costume of the day, he actually looks like Malcolm X. Denzel was a regular guy between takes when he would sign autographs and take pictures with fans.

Bespectacled director Spike Lee was known to be outspoken and, at times, anti-police in his pronouncements. Yet, when he met us, he offered a friendly hello and a handshake. He was no dope. With the massive crew and potential for numerous crowds and street shots, he needed the police at these locations.

Actor Peter Boyle was in the film, cast as a New York City Police captain. He was gracious about pictures and did not remember a previous and unpleasant encounter I'd had with him. It happened months earlier, on York Avenue on the East Side. A movie crew needed traffic held in front of one of the elite buildings in the area. We decided that the flow of traffic was just too much, so we closed off the street by the building with a couple of police barriers.

Suddenly, a small car pulled up close to one of the barriers, and the driver immediately began honking his horn.

"I have to get in there, Officer!" Peter Boyle shouted, his bald head sticking out of the window.

"They're filming a movie, and they're right in the middle of a scene," I responded.

"I don't care, Officer, I live right there, and I have to get in and bring my car up to the entrance."

"I'm sorry you can't…"

"Don't you know who the hell I am?" he shouted.

"Yes, I do, but I just can't let you drive right through the set."

"But I live right there!"

After overhearing the commotion, a young production assistant walked briskly over and saved me from further aggravation.

"Peter, Peter," the assistant said. "Peter, you of all people know the problems of shooting here."

He was a former law student turned production assistant. Did he need this? Then again, pick your poison.

"Yeah, Yeah," Boyle lamented.

Then the actor backed his car up and roared away like a teenager proud to hear the shrieks of his tires skidding.

***

I was still in movie-land, waiting outside on an interior shot, when I heard someone say, "Hey, Officer, how are ya?"

I turned and said hello to actor Ron Silver. The set was in a restaurant where the French doors were wide open for the curbside appeal. I was outside on the sidewalk where Silver was between takes for his part in Mr. Saturday Night. He was hanging out with members of the crew, having coffee and shooting the breeze. This was an easy one; remember? He said hello first. I remember that he had this wonderful theatrical voice.

When "cut" was called and folks started bustling about, I moved inside and said hello to actress Helen Hunt, then asked her for a picture.

"Sure," she said.

I already had a photo with Billy Crystal, so there was no need to bother him again, even though he looked great in character as the old comic, Buddy Young.

When the crew resumed filming, I retreated to my post outside. Matthew Broderick was walking his dog past the set when I got his photo. However, his dog did not make the cut.

***

The Distinguished Gentleman was filming at the South Street Seaport, Battery City, and the boat docks. I felt that Eddie Murphy was unapproachable, so I did not bother to ask for a picture. He walked with a swagger, as if he owned a fight, and walking beside him were three unhappily featured burly companions. Murphy was a big star, and he moved around with no peripheral vision, even when his fans called loudly to him.

Indeed, there was an incident during the shooting involving Murphy's bodyguards. I wasn't there, but apparently an autograph seeker got too close to the star, so the husky bullies threw that person into the nearest bushes. I wished we had been there. It would have been great to bust their balls. That's the problem with the celebrity-hired hangers-on. They think it's all for real, like they were guarding the President.

Sure, the more popular the celebrity, the more that person needs to feel secure from rushing fans. However, they should hire more professional people.

Also in the film with Murphy was comic-actor David Alan

Grier, who was friendly and even quirky when we got our pictures. Another co-star was the very beautiful Halle Berry. And I have a treasured picture with her.

***

Daily call sheets on a Woody Allen production were entitled, "Unknown." He would either keep the title a secret or obsess over it later. Woody was good, but stoic, when we grabbed him for a photo. His female leads in his recent endeavor were Emily Lloyd and Juliette Lewis. I got two more quick photos of them. Actually, they both played the same part. Lewis replaced Lloyd after it was rumored that Woody fired her. They were both cute, so, physically, it didn't matter. Allen looks in life as he does on film, a dour-appearing soul in baggy clothes and glasses.

One thing about Woody, he possesses the knack of painting New York as his city. He is the quintessential New York director who takes full advantage of his budding romantic landscape. All except tunnels.

Word was that "The Woodman" was too paranoid to film in claustrophobic surroundings. Maybe he thought the tunnel would implode, leaving him no way to avoid a terrible drowning death. That other famous New Yorker was also back—Robert De Niro was filming with Jessica Lange; it was a movie about a down-and-out boxing promoter. I couldn't wait to meet one of my favorite actors, especially after having blown my chance when he was in town doing Awakenings. I realized, just when I thought I might see the last of a celebrity, that they would pop back in town again, especially those who were from New York, as they loved shooting in the Big Apple.

***

In the meantime, there were a few photo ops on West End Avenue. A psychological drama was in production with Anne Meara and Anthony LaPaglia. I told Anne it was great because I also had a picture with her husband, Jerry Stiller.

That week, something interesting happened. I was assigned to a documentary about the shooting death of the famous Beatle, John Lennon. The shoot was on the West Side in a circular courtyard of a deluxe old, gray building that was eerily similar to the donut courtyard of The Dakota, where Lennon lived. Obviously this wasn't top-notch filmmaking, or they probably would have been able to actually secure The Dakota, itself.

I was sitting across the street on a stone handrail, enjoying a cigarette, when a gentleman approached me carrying an 8 x 10 manila envelope under his arm. The man had long, bushy hair and a beard. After a few minutes of conversation that I did not initiate, I found out he was a diehard Beatle groupie.

"I heard they're filming Lennon's death," he said.

Here we go, I thought, another psycho.

"Yeah, I believe that's what it is," I responded, forcing myself to adopt a conversational style.

"You know, I was there," he said.

"Interesting," I replied, though I was not really interested.

Then he pulled a couple of photos from the manila envelope. My interest was piqued when I glimpsed the first photo of John Lennon and Yoko Ono, standing in front of The Dakota. It appeared to have been taken the same night as the assassination because, in the second picture, the couple is wearing the same clothes when Lennon is signing an autograph for Mark David Chapman, the singer's murderer.

"Those are really something," I said. "It must be really eerie for you."

"I'll never forget it; ever," he said, almost shaken.

And so was this guy's brush with celebrity. His obsession that followed him years later remained in that envelope like a prized painting. It was something I sometimes feared about my own collection of pictures.

Scene XXVI

As in any other business, the movie industry possessed its fair share of gripes. There was always someone infiltrating the production and trying to hustle a piece of the pie that did not belong to them. There was one very shady character who would appear now and again on movie sets all over the city. His name was Mustafa. His claim was that he represented a group of African-American workers whose main complaint was that there were not enough jobs in the film industry for its members.

Mustafa usually showed up wearing a long, brown, leather jacket and a big fedora on his head, looking more like a pimp than a labor representative. One group he would not intimidate was the teamsters who would, in no uncertain terms, tell him to fuck off. But the teamsters did not get involved if the artsy-fartsy world of film production was going to entertain Mustafa's muscling.

Mustafa would approach the production people and remind them that, if there were no jobs, even in the lower end of the business, then he certainly could not be responsible for any hindrances to the shooting schedule that might occur, be it protests or other means. Of course, "other means" were never explained. Yet, he told the movie crews, if the company were willing to pay a salary to him, equivalent of a day's pay, everything would be acceptable. Yeah, right! Sure enough, there were enough politically correct—or maybe just frightened enough—film companies that would foolishly pay the man. All that did, so far as I was concerned, was to keep the extortionist in business. Ironically, the film companies would first attempt to put us on the spot, hoping we would solve their problem. They wanted the NYPD to get Mustafa off their backs. However, once we explained to them that they would have to draw up formal complaints, they backed off from requests for our assistance and simply paid up, forgoing any further advice.

These were often the same film crews that would ask us to get rid of any supposed derelicts lingering by the set but, when we informed them that vagrants also had rights, the same crew would allow them to peck at the craft service table. Figure it out. I always thought productions should have just paid the teamsters extra to keep certain elements away from the set.

***

My next assignment was Night and the City. After breakfast one morning, Officer Sorkorski and I were moseying around the crew campers on 175th Street and Broadway, when suddenly, from one of the trailers, Robert De Niro emerged. The New York actor stepped off wearing a tan, vested dress suit. He was in character as the would-be boxing promoter.

'Ski approached De Niro with ease.

"Hello, Mr. De Niro," he said.

'Ski was great with the initial opening. Had he been as star-struck as I was, he would have amassed a photo collection to rival that of Officer Capezzio.

"Hi, fellas. How are you guys?"

"We're good Mr. De Niro," 'Ski said. "Do you mind if we get a quick picture with you?"

"Sure," De Niro responded, patting Officer 'Ski on the back. "You guys are wearing your vests I hope? Make sure you always wear them."

I thought that was so cool of De Niro to show support for our safety. I went first, my nerves getting the best of me. I jumped in close to the actor, practically elbowing him in the side just as he was about to throw his arm around my shoulder. A celebrity with his arm around you always made the picture look more personal. But I had left De Niro no comfort zone.

So, the actual picture might appear as if De Niro was a little annoyed about being asked. Truth was he was gracious, and it was just another screw-up on my part. Again, this type of behavior amused 'Ski.

"You are too much!" he said. "Why don't you just knock the guy over? I just hope my picture comes out with your shaky hands holding the camera."

***

Later in the week, Night and the City took its cameras downtown in one of the small alleys in Tribeca. Jessica Lange was on that night, but instead of having her go back and forth to a camper, production had planted her in one of the rooms on an empty floor in the building they had rented. So, we had to lie in wait by a service elevator that was behind a stairwell on the first floor where they would escort her out to the alley.

When we received word that she would be coming to the set any minute, we headed to the small vestibule where Ms. Lange emerged, and we got our pictures with the desirable actress.

***

Night and the City filmed many scenes in an old pub in Greenwich Village on Barrow Street, which was a known hang out for the boxing community, reporters, and the like. It was there that I was to get a few more photos. There was the director, Irwin Winkler, famous for producing Rocky. There were cast mates and character actors, like cigar-smoking comedian Alan King, Jack Warden, a familiar movie face with his gruff voice, and Cliff Gorman. One day, between takes, Mr. Gorman was hanging around smoking a big, fat cigar. I asked for a picture.

"Sure," he said putting the important arm over my shoulder. Oh, boy!

When the snapshot was taken and he released his arm, the upper part of his neat silk shirt caught on my shield, causing a slight run in the material.

"Shit!" he said.

He rubbed his sleeve a few times and that was it. With his deep-set eyes, he looked like the type of guy who would have made further comments, but he didn't make a big thing out of it. I apologized, but felt like a jerk.

Demure actor Griffin Dunne walked by the set and asked me what they were filming. I told him and then, of course, I asked for a picture. The beautiful actress Susan Walters also happened by carrying her baby like a papoose on her back. She was nice about taking the photo, even though she was clearly in a hurry.

***

One night, standing in front of the bar, I got really bored and decided to take a little stroll away from the set. I ventured a couple of blocks into the village off 6th Avenue and walked by Grandpa's restaurant and peeked through the window. It had just started raining when I spotted Grandpa Munster himself, Al Lewis. When I knocked on the glass, Mr. Lewis came to the front with a look of annoyance on his face. Perhaps I knocked too hard, because I could not imagine Grandpa Munster getting annoyed.

"What's wrong, Officer?"

"Ah, nothing. I just thought you wouldn't mind taking a picture?"

What balls on my part!

He hesitated, then said, sounding like Grandpa again, "Oh, sure. I just thought something was wrong."

Thank goodness Grandpa didn't turn me down because, as I mentioned, The Munsters was one of my favorite shows.

Scene XXVII

With the holiday season approaching, Manhattan had every advantage on display — brilliant clusters of decorations and bright lights glowing like large strings of pearls. There was no equal for the film backdrop of Home Alone 2. New York was lit up during the holiday season, and Home Alone 2 used this to its full advantage.

The film included shots of Wall Street, Central Park, Battery Park, across Midtown, and up to Columbus Avenue (Columbus was also the director's name), the ornate Rockefeller tree, the Tiffany snowflake, and the colors of Christmas shining brightly from the Empire State Building.

Macaulay Culkin, who became a household name after the first Home Alone, was also the big star in the sequel. Everywhere the young actor went, so, too, did a small entourage ready to jump however high he wanted on his mere whim.

One PA put it this way, "He's the biggest star in the world right now."

For the studio, the kid was more than a star, he was a commodity.

He was also the biggest brat. I guess if I were a famous, cute 12-year-old who could have adults at my beck and call, I probably would be bratty, too. That said, on days that the camera did not actually have to glimpse Macaulay's profile, production would use a diminutive stand-in to accommodate distant and back shots as well as for camera setups in which the double stands in on a drawn line until the director feels the angle is just right. This is not meant to slight the actor, because most motion picture crews require a second unit filming and a second unit director who heads up the film's scenery and objects, along with the body doubles. It all saves time on location shots. However, if a viewing audience centered in on the actual physical work of the actor and the notion that production was always concerned about annoying Culkin, I think it would take away from the movie-going experience.

For instance, when the Culkin character is on film yelling from a taxi on the 59th Street Bridge, the actual yelling was done off camera, and the actual person in the long shot was not Culkin. Same with the Battery Park scene, where the kid is looking through a periscope at Lady Liberty or sitting on the huge bronze bull down on Wall Street. These scenes were all filmed with a double.

Granted, it was brutally cold during the shooting schedule, but I know when I saw the finished product I was bothered. That would be with any film I was aware of when viewing it from behind the scenes. I had moments when I would long for the magic of Hollywood, where the unknown intrigued me. When I could laugh, cry, root for, or hate the character on screen and not the celebrity persona.

Anyway, the crew absolutely kissed Culkin's ass. It seemed that everything on the Home Alone 2 set was at the behest of the actor.

"Mack, can I get you anything?"

Again, these are reasonable questions for a working crew, but one would have had to have been there and actually judged the tone to know the extent of the sucking-up language.

"Mack are you too tired today?" or "How you doing today, little buddy? Are you sure?"

Sometimes, the crew would even remind each other, "Leave the kid alone, he's on the phone," or "He isn't ready yet, give him more time."

And all along, I thought the director was the boss.

"Is Mac in a good mood today? Make sure he has everything he needs."

I know I shouldn't throw stones but, again, there is my paradox. Not only did I witness such foolishness, I participated in it.

Production campers were parked under the 59th Street Bridge for the readying of the taxi scene. The double was in the cab for the long shots while Macaulay stayed back playing games and watching TV in his camper without the need for supervision. Some of the officers were chomping at the bit for a photo op. Capezzio stood by the camper seriously trying to coax Culkin out for a picture. The kid was toying with Capezzio, sticking his head in and out of the window.

"Yes, no, yes!"

Then he would jump on the big dashboard and run back and forth in the camper.

Capezzio would not relent.

"Are you a real cop?" Culkin teased.

"Yes," Capezzio answered with a smile. "Come on out for a quick picture."

"Is that a real gun? If it is, let me see it!"

I actually thought Capezzio would give in and let the kid see his weapon. He would do anything for a photo. Weeks later, the kid heaped further humiliation on Capezzio by winging a snowball right at Capezzio's head, knocking his police cap off. Everyone thought that was so cute. Eventually, Capezzio was awarded his photo op.

So, it was back under the bridge where Capezzio failed that day to get his snapshot because his tour was finally over. There I was, with hours to go before the end of my shift, leaving myself open for embarrassment. Culkin eventually emerged from the camper with a female caretaker in tow. No one was around, so I decided to attempt the unusual.

"Macaulay, can I get an autograph for my nephew?"

It really was for my nephew, who was around the actor's age, and who was so cute and so similar to Culkin that he could have played the part himself. He often imitated the burning shaving lotion from the first movie, which he loved.

"Not right now," Culkin said. "Maybe later."

After he waved me off, I felt about as big as he was.

And to top it off, his crusty caretaker had to chime in, "No pictures or autographs today, OK, Officer?"

Embarrassed is putting it mildly. I was disgusted and annoyed with myself that I, a man in uniform, would stick around the movie unit for silly moments such as this. It was becoming all too idiotic.

The production staff for Home Alone 2 announced it was going to throw a pre-wrap party at Planet Hollywood in New York City. The Movie Unit was invited and, forgetting my discontent, I became a flip-flopper once again, convincing myself that the excitement of movie making was really in my blood.

When Christine and I arrived at Planet Hollywood, I was offered an impressive entrance, being able to pass by the usual line at the front door and enter through the side with my name on the guest list. The party was in the first room off to the side of the restaurant, closed off to everyone but the cast and crew of the movie. Some major players were easily recognizable.

There was Joe Pesci, down-to-earth Daniel Stern, and director, Chris Columbus, who looked like a college junior. They were all cavorting with members of the crew.

It was a sight to behold, especially in a room that was filled with fantastic movie memorabilia. There was an impressive life-like figure of Arnold Schwarzenegger as The Terminator, and encased in glass were Sylvester Stallone's boxing gloves from Rocky. Another glass case housed the bomber jacket Robert De Niro wore in Taxi Driver, and still another held the creepy doll from the Chucky movies.

With GoodFellas under his belt, Joe Pesci was the star of the moment.

Our tough-talking Italian boss was so excited that he mouthed to his wife, "Hey, dere he is — Pesch."

Pesci already had a few people huddled around him, and he looked every bit the gangster, wearing a long, wool coat and smoking a big cigar. The actor was friendly to everyone who wished to say hello and, for a moment, the cops of the Movie-TV Unit were a little bit Hollywood.

A short time later, the party retired to the lower level of Planet Hollywood, where there was a large private screening room. Imagine, a movie theater in the basement! Impressive stuff. Finally, Culkin showed up, and he immediately took the spotlight, as production people scattered from what they were doing and, like flies attracted to shit, they were up his ass in a second. There they were, those annoying, condescending voices again.

"We can't wait to see you on screen!"

"I'm sure you were just great."

"How are you, little buddy?"

There was going to be a screening of a small segment of the film that was already "in the can," in other words, finished filming. First, the kid actor and his child relatives had to be appeased with a viewing of their favorite cartoons.

Before the lights dimmed and any seats were occupied, Capezzio sensed the urgency of now or never, and he sprang into action. He gathered the Movie Unit cops (me, Wallach, Ganza, Torino, and Lanny) with our wives and dates to the middle row of seats where Culkin and a kid were a few rows up, clowning around.

Sounding like a member of the crew, Capezzio said, "Look, the kid looks like he's in a good mood. Grab your wives; let's go!"

Capezzio led the way down the aisle till he was right next to Culkin. He told his wife to sit next to the actor and charm him, "Our kids are so and so…how old are you? etc…"

Christine had gone to the ladies' room, and I began to panic.

Finally, she came out, and I grabbed her by the hand, "Where the hell were you? C'mon, everyone's getting pictures."

"Relax," she said. "Look at you guys!"

Christine was the smart one, because she couldn't have cared less about pictures or celebrities. I, on the other hand, had wanted in, even though I maintained a thousand times that I was fed up. Christine knew this conflict inside and out.

I would sneak a look at her. She thought she might have to move on.

We all got our pictures taken with the young star after a tedious regimen of begging him back towards us, as he would intermittently jump over the seats from row to row with his buddy.

If it weren't for Capezzio, none of us would have gotten any pictures.

I also coaxed Christine to take a picture with Daniel Stern, who was mingling with the folks. Next was Pesci, but by then she begged off, saying the whole picture thing had become ridiculous and embarrassing. She was right. Hell, there were times in my own life when I just didn't want a camera in my face. I remember getting annoyed at family events when relatives probably thought I was discourteous because, after a while, enough with the pictures!

Overall, it was a great experience and, knowing my love for movies, Christine bought me Planet Hollywood shorts and hats on the way out. I wondered what she was really thinking.

***

The New Year turned to shit. In Union Square Park at night, it was bitterly cold. Maybe it just felt that way because I was always outdoors. I wore my heavy sweater over my police shirt along with the issued dickey (a foot-long turtleneck that hung to the bottom of the chest worn under the duty jacket), and I was still freezing.

The low budget was turning into a slow budget, but then, luckily, the shoot wrapped early. I couldn't wait to get to my car.

To my disgusted surprise, someone had broken into the trunk of my car, swiping everything but the spare tire. All my personal belongings, including vintage cassette tapes, a bag with some clothes, and my trusted camera that I usually had tucked in my back pocket, were gone. In that camera, I had an undeveloped roll of film with pictures of Alan Alda, Jack Warden, and Jill Clayburgh. Fortunately, I would get another shot at Alda and Warden, but I never saw Ms. Clayburgh again, which was unfortunate because Jill Clayburgh was in the sisterhood of great New York actresses, along with Meryl Streep and Diane Keaton.

The car incident just gave me another reason to be totally disgusted with the city and its cretin-like inhabitants.

***

By the end of January, I was walking around with disposable cameras. I didn't want to buy a new one because I really thought I would be out of the Movie Unit soon. On Lafayette Street in lower Manhattan, there is a sandy, tan edifice, the Puck Building, that houses a huge, ballroom-like room on the first floor. A lot of commercials are filmed there, and the one I was assigned to was for Hanes underwear.

Not a very big deal until I found out that supermodel Carol Alt was on set. She breezed right past me with a smile and a hello, and I knew from friends that she would be ripe for a picture. Since I was alone, I waited for the opportune time and, as I had in the past, I goofed.

There were no dressing rooms on the set, so the model had to change behind a curtain. Boy, was I tempted to see how those Hanes looked on her; however, I was in uniform, and that would have been awkward to explain. Unfortunately, during the few hours I was there, I could not round up anyone to take a snapshot of me with Ms. Alt. It was another failure.

***

During those first few weeks of the year, it was commercials, rap videos, and parking summonses. Summons duty was usually assigned in Astoria, Queens, close to our home base.

Astoria usually gave us the opportunity to drive by Silvercup or Astoria Studios, where maybe some celebrity was hanging around. One morning, we caught up with radio personality Don Imus in his studio office. The uniform, of course, gained us access once again.

When we walked in, Imus joked, "Hey, am I in trouble or

something?"

"No," Capezzio laughed. "We just want to get some pictures with you."

Over at the Silvercup Studios, we collected photos with Phylicia Rashad of The Cosby Show, and the beautiful Vanna White, who was a guest on an early-morning talk show.

With the low activity of winter, my attention span was waning. Even the rumors were starting to bore me and, like I said, they came from everywhere, including a couple of off-duty fireman I met who moonlighted as bodyguards.

"Warren Beatty is a lunatic."

"Demi Moore has her assistant sign her autographs on 8 x 10 photos."

"Pacino loves Jeeps." I already knew that one.

"This one's maids…"

"It's multiple housekeepers, nannies, and dog-walkers… "

So, did it mean that all those photo shots of stars as hands-on parents and pet lovers were exaggerated? Who knows?

Soon, even taking photographs became less intriguing, especially if I was on a shoot by myself. I sometimes felt that I just didn't want to bother anyone anymore. It became clear that I would need the motivation of Officers Capezzio and Sorkorski. Maybe a really big feature film would cheer me up a bit.

Scene XXVIII

As if my prayer was answered, in came Scent of a Woman. Officer Ganza's words proved to be prophetic. With Pacino back in New York, I realized that I had seen the actor so many times that we should have been friends.

Al Pacino was, of course, the center of the movie, and some whispered that he was the one in charge of the whole production. Al was playing a retired and blind Army colonel whose life would experience a reawakening with the help of a college student played by Chris O'Donnell.

Many of the movie's scenes were filmed in and around the famed Waldorf Astoria Hotel on Park Avenue.

Filming in front of the Waldorf was like filming in front of The Plaza—one never knew who might happen by. During the early shots, the crew needed traffic held because they were utilizing their hydraulic mechanism to lift the camera up and pan down from the street to capture an in-and-out shot.

Suddenly, our sergeant appeared and told us that, within the hour, we would have to cease the filming and halt traffic in all directions because First Lady Barbara Bush was leaving a banquet in the Waldorf. She would be exiting through the side entrance to enter her waiting limo.

As Mrs. Bush walked into the street, surrounded by Secret Service, she waved to the crowd and flashed her grandmotherly smile to onlookers, who reciprocated with applause. Even the filming of a major motion picture halts for the government.

The director of Scent of a Woman was Martin Brest, who wore

rimmed glasses and seemed like he had a quirky personality. Brest was familiar with the crew and accommodating for pictures, as was young actor, Chris O'Donnell, who scored the role of a lifetime playing Pacino's young sidekick. Quirkiness aside, I believe all directors are geniuses.

It is no easy task to string a motion picture together, especially when the film is generating enormous positive buzz. Directors are masters of their universe. That's why many actors pursue the art of directing.

There was already talk about Academy Award nominations, especially for Pacino, who had been denied the statue for far too long. Ironically, this was the one-year I didn't think Al Pacino should have won the award. Denzel Washington was brilliant in every way as Malcolm X.

The cold lingered on in New York but, fortunately, many of the Scent of a Woman shots were interior at the Waldorf. One scene, shot in the ballroom, was the famous tango dance between Pacino and petite actress Gabrielle Anwar. Again, I failed in the photo department.

The annoying thing about the film process is that, when the camera is rolling, there must be total silence on the set. Sometimes, they demand quiet even when the camera isn't rolling. There has to be no interrupting the flow of artistic energy. For this shoot, the cameras were situated in the back of the great room and up off the ballroom floor. I stood behind one of the cameras when the dance scene was shot. I became increasingly bored with the interminable silence, so I decided to stroll the hotel corridor.

On the same floor, there was a conference room, and I heard loud chatter coming from that area. The door was open, and I decided to take a peek. A number of people were scattered about in a disorganized manner, which probably meant that whatever had been going on was now over. In the group, I spotted comedian Robert Klein and entertainer Ben Vereen.

I walked close to the stars, and, when I felt I wasn't intruding, I said, "Hi, fellas."

Both were friendly, making it easy for pictures.

Ben Vereen got a kick out of putting his hands behind his back. "Do you want to make it look as if you're arresting me?"

We all laughed, and I replied, "No, no, a picture would be fine. Thank you very much, guys."

"Our pleasure," they replied.

Satisfied with my conquest, I moseyed on back to the Scent of a Woman set in case anyone was looking for me.

Later, Pacino and O'Donnell shot a scene where they had to cross Park Avenue. Pacino as the blind man was holding a walking stick and waving it frantically as they crossed the street. He attempted this in character, unable to see where he was going. Stunt cars filled Park Avenue, blowing their horns and screeching their tires. It was risky, as stunts always are. Pacino made it to the center isle on the Avenue and then tripped into one of the decorative planted bushes.

He collided with a waiting branch that caught his eye and scratched his cornea, so the shooting scenes involving Pacino had to be halted for two weeks.

In the meantime, Martin Brest filled his calendar with long shots of the red sports car used in the film. The gorgeous Italian automobile had Pacino's double in the driver's seat.

In the movie, Pacino's character is seen as a liberated kook driving blindly—no pun intended, through the streets of New York. Of course, when Al is behind the wheel for closer shots, the car was pulled by a tow rigged with camera mounts to capture the different angles.

The car clips with Pacino were mostly filmed on the cobblestone streets under the Brooklyn Bridge.

***

Between takes one day, Al was climbing out of the auto and nearly fell on his face. A young teamster captain (who happened to be an ex-cop) was right there to break his fall. Pacino actually laughed, and there was a great moment to grab him for yet another photo. I squeezed the camera tightly in my pocket. Should I? Once again, I neglected to act on an opportunity. I failed big. It was another thought to run with for way too long.

Hey, it wasn't all bad; I got a hat that day with the movie's logo on the bill. Many productions gave out hats or T-shirts. I wanted badly to have it autographed by Pacino, but that just did not happen.

***

As time dragged on, even Scent of a Woman could not convince me to hang in there. The bottom line was, photographs aside, I was totally bored. I never would have any access to the famous other than what I was accustomed to, nor would the other cops in the unit, no matter how hard they tried.

I was anxious for a way out, but I didn't want to piss my boss off because it didn't look good if somebody wanted out of such a sweet detail.

I called Christine from work. "I've had it with this shit. Call your father…I can't believe I didn't take that picture with Pacino."

I'm sure Christine was still deciding what to do with me, but she was gentle, nonetheless. "What are you worried about? You have the picture you want with Pacino as The Godfather—your favorite movie. Listen, you're getting out of that unit, just give it time. And when you finally get out, I don't want to hear it anymore. You do realize you've complained about every assignment you ever had, and you don't realize how good you've had it the Police Department."

"Yeah, yeah," I replied.

"I'll give you yeah, yeah."

Then she let out that quiet and comforting laugh that made me feel like I knew everything was all right with us. Even still, I brought up the picture again when I saw her that night, as I would often re-examine events I already mentioned to her. She looked like she wanted to scream.

The Waldorf had a suite set up for Pacino, so he didn't have to bother with a trailer. Between takes, celebrities who wandered by, such as John Goodman and Robert Klein, would be ushered up to Al's private quarters. Even a certain famous slash victim, a model, who had probably never met the actor, was ushered in by Pacino's bodyguard after the visit was OK'd.

Scene XXIX

To an outsider ogling in, our famous Movie Unit looked as if it were the job of a lifetime. Certainly, we weren't thrust into dangerous situations, and we did get to meet hundreds of film personalities, no matter how briefly.

For the regular Joe, brushes with stardom are few and far between. Many have said they saw so-and-so from afar or from a car, or on a plane, and that was enough to thrill them.

Contrary to belief, the job was often tedious and, many times, I reminded myself of the boring sacrifice I was making for an occasional photo. The chance of a fleeting moment with an A-list actor was becoming scarce. Yet, my mind swung in forward and in reverse so many times that I was unable to pull the plug.

March arrived — not as a tamed lion — but rather as a roar of blistering cold. Between Scent of a Woman and summons assignments, I managed a few photo pickups.

The old school comic, Freddie Roman, looked like a typical Catskills jokester from way back. He was filming a promo for his live production on Broadway. We waited in the lobby of the theatre on West 46th Street between takes because of the cold.

Freddie Roman joked to me, "I'm so cold. A Jew in the Arctic."

***

The air remained chilled, but pictures were still in order, with Law and Order's Richard Brooks and soap queen Ilene Kristen.

I was hoping for a sign of spring, but it wasn't encouraging standing in the middle of Times Square on a windy and damp rainy night. It was 2:00 a.m., and the streets were uncommonly quiet, like a ghost town. The production appeared to be a small one, and the night looked as if it were going to go on way too long, although Officer Stein, with his mellow tone, was always up for good conversation, often reflecting on women he had, could have had, or should have had.

The director showed up first; his visage was very artsy fartsy. He was sizing up 42nd Street, spying camera angles through the width of his hands, viewing up at the glazed lights in the square. He informed Officer Stein and me that he was just going to shoot a short clip for his latest music video. That perked us up a bit, because Stein was a huge music fan, and he figured the dreary night might provide at least something good.

His name didn't ring a bell, but the director told us it was Phil Joanou.

I asked stupid questions to make idle conversation. "Ah, you're the director? How are you? You do music videos?"

Obviously, they were all questions I already knew the answers to.

"Yes," he said. "But I also direct movies. I directed Final Analysis."

"Wow," I said. "How was it to work with Richard Gere and Kim Basinger?"

"Richard was very cool. And Kim? Well, she's absolutely beautiful."

"Who's in this video?" I asked.

"U2," he said.

The famed Irish band had just finished playing a concert in Philadelphia, and they were scheduled to arrive in Times Square about 3:00 a.m. This was good news. Right on time, their bus rolled in to 44th Street. Lead singer, Bono, wearing his dark trademark glasses, and his crew stumbled off the bus, obviously charged and perhaps filled with liquor from a night of performing and partying.

Somehow, the group maintained a lively and good mood, despite the long night and bad weather. We took photos under a large production umbrella. It seemed as if Times Square was all ours.

Scene XXX

Christine was out of town on a business trip to London, so it afforded me more time to digest my situation. I was happy for her; she was going on her first trip for work and was somewhat excited.

After an eternity of procrastination, I finally and officially asked out of the Movie Unit. I suppose, like anything else in life that reaches an unavoidable conclusion, I had just maxed out. I was fed up with road work and traffic, tired of standing around on long nights by myself, bored with commercials and rap videos, and even tired of snacking at the craft service tables, which, along with the inactivity, was causing me to gain weight.

The boss in my Unit, the lieutenant, and the cops, all seemed to be in disbelief. I had talked about leaving, but no one thought I would really opt out. They were still surprised at my decision, even though they had listened to my griping about the job for three years. Who would want to leave such a desired Unit within the police department? And, if that weren't bad enough, who would want to return to patrol, which was considered going backwards to the bottom of the barrel? Patrol always took the grief for the department. Shit rolls downhill.

The lieutenant was livid that I wanted to leave his precious flock. It wasn't that he gave two shits about my career; it just made him look bad in the eyes of his superiors. It was simply unheard of for a cop to leave a "Hook" detail and return to patrol. Another detail would have been acceptable, but not patrol.

The lieutenant feared his boss would say, "Why is one of your guys leaving? And to patrol no less? What's the problem?"

I sugarcoated my reasons the best I could. I certainly did not want them to be too angry, then they would transfer me to any damn precinct that they wanted to out of spite. I decided to give them an explanation that would be hard for them to rebut. I told the boss I wanted to get back to the business of being a real police officer. With all that was going on in New York—crime, riots, and everything else—I said I wanted to be part of the solution again. Hey, whatever bag of shit I had to throw.

I became an actor. "You know, Lieutenant, I want to get back to being what a cop is all about. I want to do the right thing. I really miss it."

How could he explain this to his boss and get retribution when all I wanted was just to be a cop?

I continued, "I lost sight of what it's like to be a cop. I'm tired of whistling in the wind, just standing around."

Still, even with all the bullshit, I expected a dose of shoddy treatment while I was still in their care. I sensed I would be assigned the most boring jobs on the calendar.

They would indirectly tell me, "You want out? Now get the fuck out!"

Sure enough, I was assigned to rap videos in the worst neighborhoods and during the worst hours of the day. The problem with the rap videos was that many of their crews—not all—were anti-police and had no problem displaying their feelings through snubs and on T-shirts. This was a time when rapper Ice-T was about to release his disgusting song, "Cop Killer."

And the commercials were hawking products no one cared about. They were filmed in Manhattan, in the middle of rush hour. There were 4:00 a.m. starts on Monday, and then 2:00 p.m. starts on Tuesday, then early again on Wednesday. I traveled uptown, then downtown, and back again. Could this have happened regardless of my situation? Sure, but it seemed my personal schedule was always totally screwed. But that was the NYPD. Standing on 119th Street and Malcolm X Boulevard, I couldn't even say what rap group was filming. All I remember is that they were torching an American flag for dramatic effect. When my supervisor arrived, I explained the situation.

He drew on his pipe and replied, "They can do that. They're within their rights; there's nothing we can do."

But cops are patriotic and become furious when witnessing anti-type sentiments like a flag burning. Still, the boss left, telling me to make sure I remained out in the street and not in the car because I was alone and this production had to be policed. Too bad Sergeant Tito wasn't working. All he wanted to do was look important and eat. He wouldn't have minded so much if I ducked out within reason.

Anyway it was damp—the kind of chill that goes through to the bones. Not to mention there wasn't much in the way of eats on low-cost productions, and searching for food in some New York neighborhoods was like finding heartburn at the end of a greasy spoon.

Even with spring and three more productions rolling in, it was tough to get my spirits up.

However, when Christine returned, she brought with her a wonderful mood and had not mentioned the whole commitment thing. Yet, I wondered why she didn't mention our relationship. Has she given up on me? I pondered, again, that maybe I should go into one of those promotion details. Settle down and work towards the Gold Shield of detective. Maybe my "Hook's" first instincts were correct.

***

The Saint of Fort Washington, starring Matt Dillon and Danny Glover, began its run with the pair depicting what it might be like to be homeless in New York. Another film in town was Three of Hearts, a romantic comedy starring William Baldwin, Kelly Lynch, and Sherilyn Fenn.

However, all the attention was swirling around Martin

Scorcese directing a major production based on the Pulitzer Prize-winning book by Edith Wharton, The Age of Innocence.

The Saint of Fort Washington was filming in Harlem when I finally received the assignment. With three productions going on simultaneously, it was tough for the office to play games with me. Men were needed where they were needed. When I got to 117th Street, Danny Glover was dressed raggedly in character as a homeless man. He was just hanging out between takes. The actor was about to shoot a scene inside an abandoned delivery truck situated between two run-down tenement buildings. The wrecked truck was supposed to be a means of shelter for his character.

Glover was extremely friendly, signing autographs and taking pictures with the crew, as well as with local residents who cheered him on. One day, I observed that the man must have signed one hundred autographs.

A funny thing happened during the filming. Glover and Dillon were under the 59th Street Bridge, on 1st Avenue, posing as homeless squeegee window-washers. Dressed in character, they were spit shining windshields of unsuspecting motorists. Some drivers actually gave the actors change; some drove off. No one recognized either actor, and we just laughed.

Three of Hearts was filming in Washington Square Park, a great location for background, with NYU on one side, gorgeous brownstones of white and brown on another, and the huge stone arch in the middle of the park. These particular brownstones have actually been used as background in many films and, on that busy block, the crew was setting up a camera crane so they could get a shot of Baldwin walking down the street from a distance. With shots such as these, the camera is not manned in a hands-on manner. Instead, it hangs from atop the crane as the cameraman works his craft from machine controls below, sort of like how one would play a video game.

The crew managed to position some traffic cones around the crane to assure a semblance of safety since they did not have permission to close the highly trafficked street. I noticed that they were having problems, so I immediately began to hold the traffic on the corner so they could position the crane. Then, realizing that holding traffic for half a day would be extremely daunting, I borrowed the crew's orange cones and temporarily closed the street off so they would be able to get their shot.

After they got the shot, William Baldwin walked over to me and said, "Hey, Officer, I really appreciate what you did. Thanks."

"No problem."

Kelly Lynch and Sherilyn Fenn were two beautiful women who took very nice photos with me. Ms. Lynch said, "I love New York Cops. I really respect you guys."

I thought that was a very nice compliment.

***

The Age of Innocence was a period film set in the latter part of the 19th century. My first day on the film was an interior shoot in an exquisite Fifth Avenue apartment. Scorcese and company were setting the scene where the architecture was just stunning; it artfully created the distant past. The day was dreary, and there was a light rain falling. When most of the crew broke for setup shots, I wandered into the building. Setup meant they were positioning cameras and hunkering over ideas for the next shot. I walked a couple of flights up the rising circular staircase until I reached the set, which was a large dining room meticulously set for an elegant dinner scene, circa 1890. Scorsese was a master of detail and totally immersed in the time period he was shooting. I looked around for Michelle Pfeiffer, Daniel Day Lewis, and Winona Ryder.

Actually, I was more concerned with the latter two, since I did not have pictures with them. The thought did cross my mind about getting another photo with Pfeiffer. She would be dressed more elegantly as a society woman in The Age of Innocence, rather than as the frumpy waitress in Frankie and Johnny. Yet, I didn't want to put the actress out after the previous experience we had with her when she stated, "Not now."

As it turned out, it didn't matter. None of the stars were noticeably around at the moment. Later in the day, I went outside for some fresh air and a cigarette (how's that for an oxymoron?). I was hanging around on the corner near the equipment trucks conversing with a couple of teamsters when Daniel Day Lewis came from the building and passed my way. His female assistant was holding an umbrella over his head when I asked for a picture.

"No, no, it's not a good time," the assistant said. Of course it wasn't, she didn't need any favors. There it was, that sinking feeling of embarrassment again, standing there like a dope in uniform, groveling. However, Daniel Day Lewis stopped and said, "It'll be fine."

I guess he respected the uniform. Michael Tucker of L.A. Law walked by the set one day, so I grabbed a picture. Still, as the days passed, I again began to slip into a rut.

***

At the Brooklyn location, Scorcese was considerate for a picture, even though one of the teamsters said Scorcese would get annoyed if I bothered him. I was especially glad to get the picture, because he is one of my favorite directors. Unfortunately, I caught only a short glimpse of Winona Ryder as she exited her trailer and hopped immediately into a waiting car. So, I failed to get a photo of her. I remember thinking how petite and innocent looking she was. I never saw her again.

Montague Street in Brooklyn Heights is a charming block lined with brownstones that are the color of clay. New York could never be duplicated again. The crew of The Age of Innocence had dressed the street to appear as if it were right out of Wharton's book. It was paved with dirt, and all the cars were period autos. I sat in one of the cars for a goofy photo.

The gorgeous brownstones are not only classic outside, but

inside as well. The architecture is complimented with high, crafted ceilings, artistic moldings, and beautifully carved banisters. They don't make buildings like these anymore; they are turn-of-the-century relics that have withstood the test of time, thus making a perfect backdrop for the movie.

The 1940's starlet, Alexis Smith, had a small role in The Age of Innocence. When I caught up with her, she was quite gracious about taking a photo, even though she was wearing a makeup smock. Because I was so enamored with old movies when I was young, I knew who all the stars were, and I was so tempted to ask what it was like working with Errol Flynn, but my insecurities and fear of prying got the best of me.

During this period, I found myself passing on a few photo opportunities when people like Claudia Schiffer, Kirk Cameron, and Dick Cavett walked by our sets. I just didn't feel like chasing them. This was telling, as I began to think ahead of my life without the movies.

Scene XXXI

It was a long and incessant winter, followed, at times, by a tedious spring; and summer was fast approaching. My transfer was close, so I was told. At least we weren't in Los Angeles where riots were breaking out over the Rodney King verdict in which the police officers accused of beating King were acquitted. The verdict announcement was center stage across the nation. This was a time of Sharpton's radical New York.

It was not a good time for a cop to try his or her hand at public relations, especially in the high-crime areas. Then again, it was always something with the media, the politicians, and the police.

One afternoon, on Park Avenue and 125th Street, a local school was dismissing the students right where I was assigned on another crappy shoot.

As a number of kids walked by where I was standing, they spit on the ground and heckled me with a brief chant of the old standby, "Pig, pig, pig!"

I was seething, but barring actually getting spit on or attacked, what was I to do without making matters worse? For some strange reason, I began to wonder if getting out of the Unit was a wise decision? What if "The Job" was spiteful and sent me to an area where I would have to listen to this shit on a regular basis? The Unit was a sweet gig, and I would never get back in just because I realized I had made a mistake. The finality of a transfer would be like the breakup of a relationship. Unanswered questions like these played over hundreds of times in my head.

Before the shit hit the fan in New York, the NYPD was trying to beef up its image. The Department had the health of the troops in mind. Tommy Lasorda paid a visit to the Midtown North Precinct to promote the weight-loss product, Slim-Fast! He joked and posed with a group of police officers, and thus began the "Slim-Fast Challenge." Slim-Fast! would donate a fair amount of its products to members of the Department who had indulged in one-too-many donuts. The goal of the campaign was to achieve a combined weight loss of 25,000 pounds through the NYPD. I lost eight pounds using the free product.

Suddenly, on the eve of the Democratic National Convention, New York was handed its own version of Los Angeles with the riots in Washington Heights. People who lived in Washington Heights were enraged over the exoneration of a police officer's involvement in the shooting death of one of its own residents.

***

Away from the drama of unrest, director Barry Sonnenfeld was shooting a picture with actor Richard Shull in Central Park. In Midtown, the comedy, Weekend at Bernie's, was in its beginning stages of filming.

While standing on Central Park West, I spotted "Gentleman" Gerry Cooney. Cooney was once a darling of boxing, and he was the heavyweight "Great White Hope."

"Hey, Champ, how about a picture?"

"No problem."

When I stopped veteran actor Richard Kiley by the park, he asked, "Why would you want a picture of me?"

"Not of you, with you. And because you are a fine actor, sir."

Kiley deserved to be called "sir." He looked like a college professor.

By playing it cool rather than resentful, I played my hand and hoped the Movie Unit would accommodate me and not buck my transfer to a good precinct in Queens. It also looked as if it were not going to happen overnight. In the meantime, I would just sit back and maybe collect a picture or two in the process.

***

Weekend at Bernie's was an amusing production; Jonathan Silverman and Andrew McCarthy, seeming like two lost college kids, spent much of the day in Midtown, dragging around the heavy dummy that resembled actor Terry Kiser. The three actors had no problem at all taking pictures, as did Barry Bostwick, who was also on set. I must admit, since my hair was turning gray, I admired the salt-and-pepper look of Mr. Bostwick's hair.

***

The soap, All My Children, was filming a very late night shot in Central Park, and I found out that actress Susan Lucci would be on set. I was eager to get a photo with the super vixen because, admittedly, I was a huge All My Children fan. However, that evening I was slow to the punch. Susan Lucci walked to her trailer and gave us a lovely smile before she ducked in.

We're in! I thought.

I also thought we would have all night for the chance. We didn't get the photo with Ms. Lucci. Another failure for me.

The setup for All My Children was deep in the park, and the campers were situated in such a way that we were totally secluded from the public. The actress might not have surfaced for the rest of our shift, but the RATS did. Rats are everywhere in New York City. I don't think the average New Yorker understands the enormity of the rat population in New York, especially in Central Park, where the infestation is unbelievable.

Standing anywhere in the park in quiet moments is sure to bring the crinkling sound of fallen leaves beneath your feet. Anywhere there is disposed-of food or garbage-can overflow, the ugly little creatures will arrive. The quiet night near the soap opera was no exception.

Immediately after the crew set up their craft service table, the foreign visitors could be heard moving about in the nearby brush, their senses picking up scents of the feast.

We confirmed this nasty fact by shining our flashlights in the grassy area where we actually saw the beady little eyes of more than a few rodents as they made their way down the knoll. Like an advancing mini-troop of tiny, voracious soldiers, they scuttled toward the table where the pickings would be plenty.

After we convinced the crew that we would certainly see more than a few rats, they moved the craft service table inside one of the campers. Some crew members threw rocks at the rodents in a failed and laughable attempt to shoo them away. The rats were there to stay; they lurked in the dark, hoping for a feast.

In New York, rats can be seen at all hours of the day, though most of them surface at night. I often saw them pilfering through stacks of garbage or running across subway tracks. I even spotted one in the dead of winter by City Hall sitting on top of a street subway grate appearing to keep warm as the steam rose from below.

On another night in Central Park, on the Upper West Side, Officer Taylor and I heard some rustling in a nearby playground. Quietly, we approached, flashlights in hand. We thought we would find some kids hanging out in the park after hours, but what we observed was a multitude of rats enjoying the playground as if they'd waited the whole day for their turn to play in the park. They were scurrying across the playground's wooded barriers, hanging out in the sandbox, and even clustered atop the tin slide. It was truly bizarre.

I wondered how the rich folks up on Fifth Avenue would feel if they knew that the sinister little rodents had taken over their children's playground each evening.

Daylight was no deterrent to the dirty, furred creatures. Assigned to the Wollman Ice Skating Rink one afternoon, I again heard that familiar cracking sound in the bushes. I turned to witness dozens of rats converging on a nearby pile of garbage. I jumped a foot when one actually ran across my shoe. I guess that rats, like pigeons, become all too familiar with the human population. They definitely are not frightened of us.

In its defense, the city tried valiantly to eliminate the growing populace of vermin. The Parks Department dumped a ton of pesticide on the ground; unfortunately, that did more harm to dogs than it did to the rats, which were immune to the poison. I was told that New York attempted to establish owls in the trees of the park, but that was numerically impossible; there are just too many rats.

Sometimes, when I was really bored, I would pass the time wondering how many rats are, indeed, harboring in the city. If I peeked in a restaurant window at night, would I see them scurrying about? In Chinatown, where the scent of old fish is always wafting through the air, would they be lurking there, waiting to go on a scavenger hunt?

Time dragged on, and the gigs I was assigned to still consisted of a fair amount of non-celeb-oriented commercials. In the meat district one afternoon, Fontaine and I were so bored that we decided to duck into a McDonald's.

Fontaine was a germ-phobic person, and he would bite his fries down just to the tip because he feared germs, even from his own hands. When he used a pay phone, he would always put his gloves on and hold the receiver away from his ear and mouth. With all the possible germs and diseases going around in the city, I couldn't blame him for being so careful.

We were especially cautious in areas like the meatpacking district, where we could only guess at how many different strains of noxious bacteria were in the area. I found this situation faintly amusing, yet I still could identify with the anxiety associated with trying to protect oneself in a dirty environment. I even found it difficult to pee in public restrooms and in filthy, smelly precinct locker rooms, however, in case of emergency, one has to do what needs to be done.

***

One late afternoon in an old cemetery off Columbus Avenue, I decided to mosey around while a small, independent film crew was shooting by a gravesite. I was glancing up and down at old graves that were no longer visited, and I noticed a couple of large mausoleums. In the doorways of these resting places were burnt candles.

As I moved in to investigate, I saw that there were also piles of chicken bones. I didn't know it then, but later learned that many such rituals go on at night in a multitude of unguarded cemeteries. The spiritual kooks are not to be denied their turf in the city.

***

Officer Williams and I were assigned to an evening commercial spot on a sidewalk opposite the famous nightspot, Maxim's. We noticed a small group gathering in front of the club's front door, so we walked over to nose around. A few of the loitering folks appeared to have 8 x 10 photos in their hands. We discovered that Robert Redford was supposed to be in the club, and some fans were waiting outside for autographs. The doorman insisted that Mr. Redford was not in the establishment. However, the ever-faithful were willing to put their time in and wait it out till closing.

The doorman did give Williams and me a heads-up. He told us that Redford was definitely not in the club, and then he spoke in a lower voice, "But OJ Simpson will be coming out shortly."

"OJ?" my partner exclaimed. "We have to get a picture with 'The Juice.' I don't care about no Redford. I wanna meet 'The Juice'!"

"Can we stand in the lobby?" I asked the doorman.

"Sure."

There was a wide, carpeted staircase in the lobby that led to still more entrances of the club. Casually dressed in a sharp suit and open shirt, OJ surfaced, acknowledging every hello and goodbye to those he passed, as if he were a politician.

Officer Williams approached OJ before he reached the exit door and said, "Hey, OJ, how are ya' man?"

"What's goin' on?" OJ responded. "How're you guys tonight?"

"Good," Williams said. "Can we get a picture with you?"

"Of course, of course."

OJ shook our hands, posed for pictures, and never stopped smiling at the folks coming and going from Maxim's.

"My pleasure," OJ said, as he took off into the New York night.

I was half expecting him to sprint, like in the old Hertz commercials he used to make.

Who knew that, in a couple of years, he would be starring in the "Trial of the Century"? Everyone had his or her own opinions about his guilt or innocence. I know of a few New York Detectives who analyzed the murder case and, if it were up to them, OJ would be on death row.

Yet, in our celebrity-obsessed world, people still flock to get his autograph. From superstars to Joey Buttafuoco, we live in an anyone-who's-recognized world.

For me, time became a mere formality. I was next assigned to beneath the West Side Highway, where there are strings of old coves and graffiti-covered band shells. A low-budget film was being shot, and the crew informed me that the lead was the kid from Boyz 'N the Hood. Even after I met Cuba Gooding, Jr., I was still confused about which actor he was. I thought perhaps he was Larry Fishburne.

Gooding would eventually gain fame after winning an Academy Award for Jerry Maguire. In the film with Gooding were two young actresses, Moira Kelly and Martha Plimpton. I told Moira Kelly that she looked like Winona Ryder.

"I get that all the time," she said. "You know, I'm actually older than she is."

We put our arms around each other and had our picture taken.

***

Downtown in Alphabet City, artsy Fisher Stevens was directing a small independent film. I wanted to ask him what it was like to date Michelle Pfeiffer, but I settled for a picture. On set with Stevens was New York character actor Rick Aviles. Some coparazzi moments were stress free.

***

Also directing downtown was Melanie Myron of Thirtysomething. Her movie starred the real Larry Fishburne and veteran actor Phil Bosco. While on set one day, I noticed a couple of well-dressed black men approach production and ask to speak with Mr. Fishburne. They weren't fans and, to my surprise, Fishburne walked over to them. Being a slightly nosey person, I managed to get an ear in and pick up some of the conversation.

The men were asking Fishburne something about the crew. They wanted to know if there were an ample number of African-Americans working on the picture. Did Fishburne, an African-American actor, think it was fair?

They definitely were not from Mustafa's gang; he usually showed up solo. And these guys seemed to focus more on the acting, while Mustafa focused on everything that would bring in a buck, even if it meant serving coffee.

I overheard Fishburne say to the men, "I'm not going to play that game with you."

I thought it was the right thing to say. Fishburne was not intimidated by them. He then seemed to be in a hurry, but he stopped for a quick picture with us. So, too, did Melanie Mayron and Phil Bosco.

***

Occasionally, every cop in the Movie Unit would get a turn at the mail-run assignment. This entailed transporting all the paperwork to and from the Movie Unit and the Mayor's Office of Film. It was actually a good assignment. It was almost like time off from the grind. If the day was slow, the cop had the choice of taking some personal time and going home early after the run was completed.

The Mayor's Office of Film was located on 54th Street in a simple, nondescript building.

The office was housed on two upper floors and looked like any other basic business office. There were little cubicles separated by glass with views of the surrounding working atmosphere, as well as a view of the West Side neighborhood. The executive offices, where the production meetings were held, were located in the back part of the main office behind closed double doors.

There is a sense of nostalgia in the office, with its posters from an earlier time of New York film shooting. Advertisements for movies such as Annie Hall, both Godfather films, Serpico, and Dog Day Afternoon plastered the walls.

On one occasion, I dropped off some paperwork to one of the secretaries whose desk was adorned with autographed 8 x 10 photos of various celebrities.

"How's everything? Blah, blah, blah...."

I left the office with the return mail in hand and went back to my car that was parked in front of the Motor Vehicles Adjudication Office, where many of the city's summonses are heard. Just as I opened the door to the radio car, I spotted the actor, Frank Vincent, and his neatly coiffed silver hair, coming out of the Motor Vehicles building. Frank Vincent is known for his roles playing mobsters in such movies as Raging Bull and GoodFellas.

"Hey, Frank Vincent! How are you?" I said.

"Hello, Officer."

"What are you up to?" (See how easy it was when I wasn't intimidated by superstardom or entourages?)

"Filming in the area?"

"No, I'm here payin' a friggin" parking ticket," he said,

laughing.

I complimented his work, and he thanked me, telling me he was working on a couple of films in the near future.

We took a photo; I wished him well, and we said our goodbyes. Nice guy.

***

That same week, HBO was starting a miniseries shoot, Barbarians at the Gate. The first scenes were in Midtown, where I spotted the actor James Garner walking from the set.

I politely asked for a picture, and he politely agreed. It was cool, because Mr. Garner had aged, of course, but he will always be a legendary movie star from the old school.

Actress Nina Siemaszko was crossing a street when I got her picture. Ms. Siemaszko had just finished another miniseries playing Mia Farrow in an upcoming Frank Sinatra bio.

***

Filming in Brooklyn, Harlem, and inside the temporary Midtown North Station House was Forest Whitaker directing his first movie. The movie was a cops-and-robbers drama starring character actors Michael Biehn, of The Terminator, and Craig Wasson of Body Double. (I wondered what had happened to him since that movie, which was a fairly successful film.) Michael Biehn told us he was happy to meet real cops.

***

Movies were back in full swing as Mr. Wonderful began its run, starring Matt Dillon, Annabella Sciorra, Mary-Louise Parker, and William Hurt. Parts of the film were shot in the Brooklyn Botanic Garden, a precious haven situated only blocks from neighborhoods that had the distinction of having high crime rates. The Garden was truly a sanctuary from those nearby streets.

I didn't need my picture taken with Dillon, but I did take one with Ms. Sciorra, who flinched when she put her arm around me as she accidentally grabbed my handcuff case. Her look was indeed ethnic and beautiful.

William Hurt was also in the Garden that day, so I assumed that, in the private setting, a picture would be easy. He seemed to be walking in deep thought, sort of like Pacino does, his head down paying attention to no one. He'd shoot a scene then head straight to his camper.

I had a bad feeling about asking the actor for a photo. He made no eye contact, whatsoever. Even though I was wearing a uniform, the lack of eye contact was not a good sign. But, hey, it was a secluded area; there were not a whole lot of folks to be embarrassed in front of, and I hadn't even grabbed anyone to take the picture for me. Yet.

When I asked for a photo, Hurt didn't even look up.

He just waved his hand and mumbled, "No, no, thanks anyway, I don't do that stuff."

Take a chill pill, I thought.

Other actors in the film—Bruce Kirby, Dan Hedaya, and Luis Guzmán, all fine character actors—participated in a group shot with me standing on the Brooklyn Promenade, the majestic Twin Towers in the background.

Guzmán was a regular guy who still lived in his old neighborhood of Alphabet City. This wasn't like the Hollywood I had imagined, the days of old, when character actors would congregate with the stars on studio lots and in nightclubs.

Scene XXXII

It was a waiting game. At least I wasn't freezing my ass off, so I just attempted to enjoy every day as if it were my last in the Movie Unit. Knowing it would all be over soon comforted me a bit.

Meanwhile, Tony Goldwyn, grandson of legendary studio head Samuel Goldwyn, was in town directing an action picture. Another shoot-'em-up, the dark drama, Romeo is Bleeding, was also in town, as was Woody Allen and his next unnamed project. Even some low-budget movies were seen filming in New York. One starred Eileen Brennan, who simply possessed the aura of a funny woman. Her costar was Adam Arkin, who seemed every bit as dour as his father.

However, it was two more photos that I nailed.

***

Again assigned to the Silvercup Studios, I was to make sure the movie campers were parked appropriately. While I was there, I caught up with actress Theresa Saldana, who was getting out of a car. She was "delighted" to take a picture. I couldn't help thinking how brave and resilient she was to have survived a real-life stalking drama in which her attacker stabbed her numerous times in an obsessive rage.

***

I was with my friend Officer Torino on the West Side docks

where Goldwyn was filming scenes for his action flick. The docks were semiprivate and still housed old boathouses. The scene entailed a barrage of machine gun fire filmed from a rolling dolly set up across the dock. It was sort of like a speeded-up duck hunt in an amusement park.

Of course, as in all films in which simulated gunfire is involved, the local precinct was notified, and a wire was also sent out on a Teletype to the rest of the city.

NYPD certainly didn't want police racing to a scene that was filled with the noise of fake gunfire; that would set up a situation that could turn into total mayhem. Between takes, Torino and I were standing opposite the water facing New Jersey as we began chewing the fat.

In the past, we had many conversations about our fortune of meeting celebrities. It was cool conversing with members of the Movie Unit about a subject that actually brought us there in the first place. Torino had some great pictures, too. That Pacino picture by the Brooklyn Bridge was the best. Shit, I recalled the time Pacino stumbled out of his car and the teamster broke his fall, causing Pacino to smile. I had the camera in my hand, and I didn't take the picture.

There was a common bond between us as we rehashed stories about people we actually met.

On this day, however, the conversation with Torino was on a different subject.

"I can't wait till I get transferred," I said.

"You should do what you think is best," he replied. "I just hope you're not making a mistake and going back to patrol and all that bullshit."

Then he turned his face and looked out over the water. "Just look at this view!"

The guys in the Movie Unit were so much less uptight than patrol cops. Torino's thoughts would turn out to be very prophetic words.

Talk turned to my relationship status, with Torino asking me when I was finally going to get married. How ironic it was, because I had been wondering quite frequently whether Christine would hang in there or if she was ready to move on.

I told him I really wasn't sure, but I was going to have to make a decision soon, or I would lose Christine. I was plainly scared to death. I could have been married twice before, so I thought I would be doomed to fail.

"The funny thing is I enjoy the little things now, the romantic things," I told Torino.

"Well, then," he said. "Let me just ask you one question."

I looked at him and smiled. It wasn't difficult to figure out what he was going to ask.

"Look, we're all afraid, but do you love her?" he asked.

"Yes, I do. And that's why I don't know what the heck is wrong with me. What if it doesn't work out?"

Why was I projecting? Was I really ready to ruin another good thing in my life?

"What if I screw things up?" I asked.

"Hey, just remember, nothing's perfect. You've heard me and my wife argue. It happens. Just get over it right away, and it'll be fine. You won't know that until you try," he responded.

I laughed. All the guys complained about their wives, but in the few social gatherings where we were all together, I could see clearly that much of it was just talk.

Still, I imagined that love should be like it is on film, a guaranteed happily ever after, with no chance of problems. But, of course, I knew that just wasn't true. As corny as it sounds, love is a journey into discovery. But this story is about celebrity, so I'll leave my love affair with Christine tucked away for now in my journals and my poetry.

I will say that when I met Christine, she was everything I was looking for. Not only was she beautiful, but also she had an ethereal softness about her. She was intelligent. (I knew right off that she was smarter than me) and funny, too. There seemed to be a depth to her soul. So, with trepidation and a prayer, I allowed myself to fall in love.

Torino and I took pictures with Goldwyn and enjoyed the rest of the day talking on the sun-drenched waterfront dock where no onlookers could infiltrate the closed-off set.

I would still find myself reflecting on the whole picture-taking process. Who was difficult? Who was cool? Did it really matter? Should I understand that it was OK for actors to just be having a bad day? Like William Hurt — maybe he just didn't feel like it.

Were some stars who were huge in pop culture required to have security? Of course.

As for me, was I really the restless soul who would always have to move on?

In retrospect, I felt like I blew it. I was given a once-in-a-lifetime chance, and I should have gone for it, pictures and autographs. What movie lover in my shoes would not have relished the opportunity?

***

Romeo is Bleeding was filming scenes inside an old tavern in Ridgewood, Queens. There were three actors on set that day, Gary Oldman, Lena Olin, and Will Patton. Miss Olin disappeared into a camper and waited until production was ready to film her sequence. Old faithful, Officer Sorkorski, managed to get photos with Will Patton and Gary Oldman. Oldman actually recognized 'Ski from a previous shoot in New York. Both actors hung around the set without fanfare or assistants. It was apparent that the less preferential the treatment, the less the ego.

***

One night in Brooklyn, the shoot went late into the evening and early morning. Production rented the second floor of an old apartment building on Myrtle Avenue in Bedford-Stuyvesant. The apartment and rooms were set up with craft services and couches so the crew would have a place to relax.

A couple of us walked up the flight of stairs to grab a cup of coffee when we noticed a female sitting on the couch arguing into a phone. One of the crew later confirmed to us that Juliette Lewis was shouting at her boyfriend, Brad Pitt. That was the guy wearing the ridiculous hairdo on another set. I laughed. Who knew?

***

Romeo is Bleeding moved to the Brooklyn piers that week to film some action sequences. There was one scene where Lena Olin, scantily clad in white underwear and garter belt, was to wrestle and fight with one of her costars. All eyes were on the lovely actress. Later, when she was dressed, I asked Ms. Olin for a photo. She still had some fake movie blood on her face, but that was fine.

***

As hot as the New York summer could be, it beat the brutal winter, anytime. Yes, at times it felt as though I could have a heat stroke in my hot uniform, especially with all the equipment we had to wear. In those days, "The Job" did not enforce the mandatory wearing of body-armored vests, which would have added ten pounds of sweat. I just had to keep drinking water.

In the interim, I was assigned to 125th Street and Fifth Avenue, where the early morning was already showing signs of being a hot, sticky day.

Oh, shit, I thought.

It appeared that I was in for another round of rap music and flag burning, complete with the usual attitude, and it was on one of the hottest days of the end of summer, too.

Boy, was I wrong! The video was for Bon Jovi and his band's latest album. Naturally, that perked us up. 'Ski, Officer Wallach, and I waited for the group to make its appearance. Our job was to walk alongside the band as they traipsed up 125th Street toward Fifth Avenue. We were supposed to stay out of the camera's eye, of course. Being the group's security was plenty for us. It was the cameraman's job to catch the ambience of Harlem and its streets, filled with peddlers selling their wares.

The crew, as they often did, thought we were in a very dangerous place. Just the name, Harlem, invoked fear. They made it known that they were very grateful to us for being there. We knew we had to be on our toes, after all, it wasn't a Hollywood back lot, it was a place where crime really was a possibility.

We had moved off the corner of 125th Street when the group began to surface, unnoticed, one by one.

"Hey, guys. How've ya' been?" It was the band's guitarist, Richie Sambora.

He made the usual small talk by sharing his opinion that, "New York cops really have it rough."

I'm sure there were those in the limelight who did sincerely think the police had it rough. But the phrase seemed all too generic.

On a quiet street where the campers were parked, we had our pictures taken with Sambora and lead singer, Bon Jovi. With the pair's wild hair and good looks, they were the quintessential rock stars.

The day went fast, especially between takes when 'Ski and Wallach brought on some cop humor by gossiping about our bosses. Basically, they tore them to shreds talking about one sergeant's rug, another one's boss whose hands actually shook because he tried to quit smoking, and another boss's ugly wife. We laughed quite a bit.

Two wrap parties were on tap, so I decided I would go because I knew it would be my last opportunity. Mr. Wonderful's wrap party was downtown in a small pub; it was very comfortable with a long bar and pool table in the rear. I went with Christine, Officer Torino and his wife and, since it was an open invite, I took my sister, Chicky, along. My siblings were representative of the stereotypical, good-looking, dark-haired sons and daughters of Queens, in manner and in speech. No, they were not like the hard-core Guidos and Guidettes who were often mocked and imitated.

My sister immediately gushed over Matt Dillon, then coaxed him into a picture and an autograph, telling the actor, "My son's name is also Matt."

Mary-Louise Parker was sitting on the front windowsill of the bar drinking a beer. She looked like any other down-to-earth, attractive lady hanging out through the night. Model Stephanie Seymour was by the pool table watching a game. The last time I saw her, we took a picture with her slender arms and fingers around my potbelly. I would have loved to impress the gorgeous model by beating one of her friends at pool but....

The bar was closed to outsiders and, once again, I felt my reward of privilege. It was all very Manhattan-like. Wow.

The Age of Innocence was a more refined party that was hosted in a fancy restaurant in the heart of Restaurant Row near Broadway. This time, I took one of my brothers, Anthony, with us, because he was dying to meet the actresses Michelle Pfeiffer and Winona Ryder. When we arrived, Daniel Day Lewis was hanging out at the bar and Martin Scorcese was sitting in the rear dining area holding his dog, Zoe. It was a quiet evening in which neither actress showed up, so we enjoyed a great meal and decided to leave.

***

Like all summers, it went too fast. The buzz for early fall was the movie Robert De Niro had chosen as his directorial debut. A Bronx Tale was originally a one-act play that was written by Chazz Palminteri. He also starred in the movie.

The story revolved around a mob neighborhood in the Arthur Avenue section of the Bronx as seen through the eyes of a young boy. De Niro just happened to see the play one night and loved it. Talk about Chazz being in the right time and the right place.

However, the film was to be shot entirely in Queens, because, as another movie rumor had it, the real mob did not want the film shot in their fabled neighborhood.

In Astoria, Queens, a long stretch of 37th Avenue would become the main set for A Bronx Tale. Storeowners and apartment dwellers were paid handsomely for the use of their respective properties. The lure of money, however, was not the only attraction for the common folk. People really believed it was a big deal if something that belonged to them was part of a movie. I guess they felt as if they possessed their own Southfork Ranch of the TV series, Dallas.

It was always nice to be on a set that transported me back to another time, especially if character style and dress were familiar. In this case, I felt as though I were in my father's Bronx, circa 1960s.

Though 37th Avenue would be closed for much of the shoot, the side streets adjoining were open to traffic and had to be policed on many occasions because motorists were stopping and honking. The novelty of Hollywood finally wore me down, and it wasn't only I, but also many of the residents of Astoria who began to feel the inconvenience of traffic buildups and noise from a shooting schedule that sometimes went late into the night.

Residents could be heard screaming from windowsills.

"Enough already!"

"Not this loud, please!"

"C'mon, will you guys knock it off!"

There was one resident who captured his own 15 minutes of fame by habitually howling his displeasure at the crew, often disrupting filming.

"WOO, WOO!" he would yell at the top of his lungs from his upper apartment in an adjoining building.

It became a lasting joke on the set, "Is the Whoo-Whoo man out there tonight?"

Even De Niro thought it amusing enough to list the Whoo-Whoo man at the end of the movie's credits.

Radioman even found his way to the set, and asked, "Where's De Niro?"

A Bronx Tale was a big enough project to warrant our entire unit getting assigned the job at one time or another.

Frequently, the shoot required at least four or five of us. If we were assigned somewhere else and that job wrapped early, there was no going home.

It was no secret that De Niro was friendly with Mayor Dinkins, so, anything the actor-director wanted, he got. But we all kind of did, as well. The shoot was a relaxed gig with many of the streets closed off.

Then there was the food. Like many major productions, they fed us extremely well, often bringing in catered meals. On this set, they often served delicious steaks, fresh salad and vegetables, good coffee, and great desserts.

The Italian-American actors on set were very entertaining to observe. These characters really thought they were mobsters. Who knows? Maybe some really were; they sure played the part on screen and off. Many of them sat around in circles playing cards wearing "Guinea tees" (sleeveless undershirts). They wore polyester slacks and talked with their hands in elaborate overstatements. Many of the actors were familiar from past De Niro movies. (A common practice in Hollywood is to work with many of the same character types who formerly worked with a familiar director or actor).

Chazz Palminteri introduced himself to us and said, "I can't believe I'm workin' with Bobby De Niro!"

I certainly would have felt the same if I had I somehow made it from a Bronx neighborhood all the way to Hollywood, and not just to any Hollywood but to De Niro's Hollywood on the Hudson. Chazz was a nice guy who just wanted everything to run smoothly. He took pictures and signed autographs for anyone who asked.

Even De Niro, who usually ducks the crowds, schmoozed the neighborhood folks with his customary courtesy; he signed autographs and allowed people to take his picture, which many store owners proudly hung on their walls, surely to brag about forever.

Many of the younger actors were fairly new to the game and

often whispered the sentiments of Chazz Palminteri. "De Niro — can you believe it?"

De Niro, following the style of his mentor, Scorsese, peppered A Bronx Tale with violence. It was interesting to watch De Niro direct his pal Joe Pesci, especially in one of the film's violent scenes where Pesci is involved in a bat-wielding, road-rage incident.

"Gunfire on set," had to be announced and reported frequently during the filming.

Besides directing, De Niro played a pivotal role in the film as a hard-working bus driver who attempts to show his son that honest work is more advantageous than being a big shot. The vintage 1960s buses were rigged with cameras that rolled as De Niro would drive down 37th Avenue past his fictional home, which was on the character's bus route.

There was another setup for a violent confrontation between Chazz's character and his boys against a wandering motorcycle gang that happens into "The Chazz Bipi." The bikers are unaware that the joint (bar) is run by Wiseguys. They become belligerent and, of course, the boys teach them who is boss. It was reported that De Niro employed some real life Hells Angels for the film.

Not only were most of the new actors enamored with De Niro, but we were, too. One day, I brought to the set an old 8 x 10 photograph of De Niro that was taken when he played the young Vito Corleone in The Godfather, Part II. One of the bus scenes took place in Astoria, which ran a fictional route through the housing projects. The timing was perfect as De Niro walked from the set to a nearby waiting car.

"Mr. De Niro? Bobby?" I called out.

He didn't seem to hear me, then that old familiar and uncomfortable feeling of embarrassment began to rear its ugly self.

"Mr. De Niro?" I said a little louder.

De Niro traveled with his bodyguard throughout the filming, an average-sized male black in his forties. Now they both turned around.

The bodyguard quickly stepped in—waving his hands between the actor and me. "No-no, Officer, not now."

I felt like shit. Here I was a New York cop, standing there in uniform, being instructed by a hired hand basically to get lost.

Suddenly, De Niro, dressed in a long down coat, stepped forward toward his man.

"No," the actor said. "It's OK, I'll sign for the officer."

From shit to shinola!

De Niro impressed the hell out of me with his respect for the uniform. He didn't know I was in the Movie Unit; it was enough that I was a cop. It was so cool and made my day. Take that, you bodyguard!

Before my eventual release from the Movie Unit, I was to have one more defining moment that had nothing to do with a photo op.

***

As I reflect on De Niro, I go back to one of his earlier roles. In the movie, Taxi Driver, De Niro played one of his most complex roles as a cynical New Yorker who harbored extremely gloomy thoughts.

Between days on A Bronx Tale, I was assigned to another commercial, something about diet soda. The shoot was in SoHo, near many of New York's art galleries situated on one of the neighborhood's many narrow streets.

With not much to do on the set, I dreamed up my own egregious Taxi Driver moment. Who knows? Maybe it was because I didn't stick to my niche. Maybe it was because I was disappointed and somehow thought the unit would be more glamorous, or that I would fall into an ostentatious lifestyle. Or maybe my attention span was in its usual self-sabotage mode. Still, maybe I was just tired of thinking about my personal and professional decisions for a moment.

I was not needed on the street yet, so I was sitting in a marked police cruiser. I was hoping no one would notice me because, even though I was in a police car, I was sitting really low in the seat. I wanted to go unnoticed because, on that day, I was feeling more than the usual cynicism. Earlier, I had driven slowly off the ramp of the Manhattan Bridge when, to the right down by 3rd Street, I noticed the encampment of a tent city, where the destitute who have no place to live construct small blanketed or tin huts for themselves and seemingly appear to live outside the Metropolis, where all the just desserts are in the hands of the privileged.

I wondered if all the bleeding hearts had, on some days, passed the same plot of land.

I was in no mood for the usual mindless questions that people on the street feel compelled to ask.

"Why are there cops here today?"

"Where is the closest bus stop?"

Questions such as these always had a way of annoying me.

The bright and early afternoon was beginning to blindside the windshield, so I pulled down the visor hoping that would make me even less noticeable. Soon the lowering sun would be glaring through the windshield, and I'd be forced to move. It was supposed to be an easy day because production was to wind down with the sun.

I was sitting low behind the dashboard wearing dark sunglasses, my eyes scanning the sidewalks. Directly across the street there was an old church, historically splendid and immaculately manicured.

As my eyes wandered over the entire building, I found the distraction I had been looking for. Lying on the extreme right steps was a middle aged man, obviously homeless, drunk, or both. For most liberals in the city, that is OK, unless of course, the street inhabitant is parked on one of their stoops.

I could never fathom why homeless people have to sprawl themselves out on the church steps as if the church were obliged to offer sanctuary. An ornament lying before God should inspire mercy? That's crap!

Does anyone think that God-fearing parishioners want to walk over a sleeping log on their way into Mass?

After a few minutes, the man tried getting up from his slumber, groping for the wall in desperation. When he finally stood as tall as he could, he reached into his pants, pulled out his pecker and began pissing on the wall of the magnificent church.

I thought, that's for all the kind-hearted folks who "ooh and aah." They pity these poor souls, believing that most of the time it's not their fault, that it's the problem of society. "These lost souls were probably on their way to becoming lawyers or doctors."

It's hard to buy that crap when watching someone piss on a church.

It's one thing if a person is mentally disturbed; it's quite another if that person is just an asshole. If I were high up on the rung of success and wound up in the gutter, I probably would save one last bullet and put a hole in my head the size of a quarter.

In any event, the guy should be dragged away for desecrating the church. I tried not to get aggravated; no one else seemed to give a shit, so I sat back viewing the whole thing as entertainment. Get involved? For what? To have someone with a cause tell me to leave him alone? Especially down in lower Manhattan. I could just hear it:

"Don't you cops have anything else to do?" (A famous line civilians use when they're receiving a ticket.) Some of these city dwellers make me want to spit in their morning coffee.

All these movie people are the same way, I thought. Always chirping about a cause that rarely mentions cancer or heart disease. What they fail to realize is that half the people they feel inclined to support are turning our cities into cesspools. But that's how liberal outrage operates, it's excuses for the disenfranchised.

As I turned my eyes to the left, I saw a crewmember approaching—obviously with a question. The guy was short and bald, and he was sporting these orange, advertising-type glasses that matched his ridiculous designer shorts and T-shirt. The only thing missing was a can of diet soda in his hand.

He started off with the usual phony greeting, "Hello officer, how are you? Did you get coffee?"

"Yes I did, thanks," I replied.

Then he started in about camera setups and angle shots. Good thing I had my dark glasses on, or he would have noticed my lack of interest. "Do you think you could help us back the small truck in?"

What the hell? I thought. He was polite. As I exited the car, he continued to speak about the commercial. What he didn't realize was that I just didn't give a crap anymore. My grandiose longing for Greenwich Village and its charming cobblestone streets was giving way to the reality of the filth that paves that fabled district.

Scene XXXIII

Soon, I learned I was going to be transferred to the 111 Precinct in Bayside, New York. Of course, nothing in the NYPD was a guarantee, but the "Hook" was in, and I was more than certain that is where I was headed. My future father-in-law, Ron, came to the rescue. I was going to be back in a heated and air-conditioned radio car in a very nice section of Queens. It would be a great commute to my Long Island home and three more years in the bank towards retirement.

No more nightmare traffic jams or worrying about where and what my assignment was. No more anxiety about who was smiling in a photo, who had their arm around me, or when the picture opportunities would come at all. No more worries about who I would decide to get an autograph from, against my better judgment. No more concern about whose signature was legible and was it authentic?

The human side of celebrity could now be better left a mystery, except for the constant babbling on news circuits from the extreme left celebrity, with their political and personal ranting that took away from their performance on screen. Well, for me, anyway. When was the last time a Republican celebrity made imprudent remarks followed by an unabashed tirade?

Elvis Presley once said, he'd rather keep his opinions to himself, that he was just an entertainer. Actors have faces; they're not writers. Much of their career is built on the premise of how they appear on screen and how that look transforms into the character they're portraying.

Thus, they should be remembered for such portrayals and

should be seen but not heard beyond the movie. That's my opinion.

When transferred, I would leave behind a feeling of expectance from a complex industry and the people who reside in its complex world. It was like my relationship with Sinatra, in which the mystery remained intact. Simply knowing the man through film and song sufficed.

I needed to enjoy myself again when it came to the movies. I have said that the exposure to the industry was making the magic of movies wear off for me. Instead of being on the edge of my seat, I would analyze the film-making and I would see again the peripheral part I played. I knew what went on behind the scenes. I would say to myself, I was there, or I met that actor, or they really weren't doing it that way, or the camera placement was.... On and on.

I just wore myself down.

During this time, George Steinbrenner was still into doing good deeds for the NYPD. COPCARE was a benefit that aided police officers and their families with support for medical and psychological problems, and the Department named Mr. Steinbrenner their Man of the Year. My own psychological situation was that I became resolved to the fact of transfer, and now I could linger through yet another film. Some problem, eh?

***

Movie goddess-of-the-moment, Sharon Stone, was making her splash in New York with the filming of Sliver, a sex-charged murder mystery. Stone was very much at her peak after Basic Instinct; her sexuality was unmatched. Her costars in Sliver were William Baldwin and Tom Berenger.

Since I already met Baldwin, I was naturally on the lookout for Ms. Stone and Tom Berenger. I figured if I were going out, it would be an ideal ending with Sharon Stone as my last photo. But, as usual, I would have to wait my turn on the new shoot. In the interim, I was sent to Gramercy Park, where Woody Allen was in production for another New York story.

Again, there were the buildings, the lush décor of colorful flowers and trailing vines. It was privacy only a block from the trafficked avenues.

As the Allen film broke for lunch, I quickly jumped at the chance to get my photo with Diane Keaton. I had adored Keaton ever since she played the pretty innocent in The Godfather.

I was still efficient at spotting celebrities. I was assigned to a location under the Williamsburg Bridge and was told it would be a quick day with no celebrities. There were two men filming a scene in an apartment doorway, and I quickly recognized one whom I had seen in an off-Broadway theater in Los Angeles; he played the role of Howard Hughes. The actor — and future nominated star — was James Cromwell, a very tall, deep-voiced man. He was surprised and delighted that I remembered the play and his role.

***

In the same week, I spotted character actor Dominick Chianese. I was in Little Italy when I walked over to him and called him Johnny Ola. Mr. Chianese was grateful that people still recognized him from that role in The Godfather, Part II. He would later become more popular as Uncle Junior in The Sopranos.

***

Finally, I got to Midtown, and Sliver. I was eager to meet Sharon Stone, because I was told my transfer would come any day now. I arrived on set fully prepared to seek out my last photo. When I saw Billy Baldwin on set signing autographs for fans, I assumed that all the stars would be on set that day.

I approached Baldwin and said, "How are you Billy? I worked with you on Three of Hearts."

"Hey, how are you, Officer?" Not that he remembered me.

I relieved Officer Torino, who told me I had just missed Tom Berenger. Torino was a fan of Mr. Berenger because, like himself, the actor was a huge Civil War buff. Torino told me he got his picture taken with Berenger, who was wearing a big Texas hat. He also conversed briefly with the actor about the new Civil War picture Berenger was going to star in. That would have been like if I'd had the chance to talk with Pacino about The Godfather, Part III. Oh, well, that was my luck.

It turned out that Sharon Stone was not on set that day, either. I was disappointed, because I believed that would be my last chance, but I put into my head that this is what I wanted, and I would soon be out of fantasyland, anyway.

*****

The next day, my transfer stalled, I was back on Sliver. I was assigned there with picture-taker extraordinaire Officer Capezzio, who signaled to me that Ms. Stone was more than likely to be on set, and Capezzio was sure to snap us some photos.

Capezzio also reiterated his thought about my wanting out.

"You're fuckin' nuts!" he said emphatically. "You're going to leave this? You love this shit like I do. You're always talking movies and stars."

"I know, but it's definitely too late now."

Ironically, I had run into a childhood friend of mine, Roland, a big guy. I was directing traffic on a soda commercial when my old buddy drove by in an oil truck. He recognized me, pulled over, and we chatted. Of course, the whole movie thing fascinated him.

"You got it made!" he told me.

"Actually, I'm leaving the Movie Unit soon," I told him.

"What? Are you kiddin' me? You always loved this shit!"

Where have I heard that before?

Remarks such as those always caused an instant, indecisive flip-flop with my obsessive emotions. Did I really make the right decision? It was easy to feel conflicted when I worked on a major motion picture. Capezzio was right. Though I tried to fight it, I was still in love with movies. How many times have I said I wasn't interested, and then some film would come into town, and I would get all warmed up again?

Should I have waited it out until I climbed the ladder of seniority, when I would be one of the top men landing the choice assignments?

As far as the assholes in the unit who were called supervisors — well, they never lasted longer than cops in one place, because they were either retiring or seeking a promotion, although I don't know why. As far as I was concerned, a sergeant in the Movie Unit had the best job in the Department.

For the sergeant, there was no sitting around in one spot completely bored, instead, he would visit cops at each movie location, where the supervisor could eat, converse with teamsters, get a photo with a celeb, and then be on his way. The sergeant also gets to attend scouting location meetings, not to mention more overtime and first dibs at the wrap parties. WOW!

Anyway, my need for rationalization still caused nagging doubts.

Beyond all the personal strife, I wondered if the film industry would, indeed, get fed up with the high costs of union bills and New York's exorbitant fees. Maybe the companies would fold up their tents and move on to Canada. Selfishly, I hoped the money situation would cripple New York filming to the extent that the Movie Unit would have to break up, and I would be let off the hook with my tough decision behind me.

Of course, that was not really going to happen. For all of the faults of New York — money, availability, aggravation — there was no better nor more perfect backdrop for casting than the ambience, real or imagined, of our city.

Sliver had its share of troubled rumors, as much as any other film. Producers were allegedly fighting; there was talk of actresses acting bitchy and demanding. Stories of affairs and bust-ups among the star, the producer, and the writer were circulating. It was just a typical movie set.

And Sharon Stone was close to appearing on set.

All I could say is that when I first laid eyes on Sharon Stone, there was no mistake in the hype, she was absolutely gorgeous and dripping with sexuality. Under a light, loose-fitting jacket, she was dressed in a V-necked T-shirt and basic gray sweatpants, still every bit a star.

Officer Capezzio was drooling. There was no way in hell that we would leave that day without pictures. Even if it were true that the actress was a bitch, Capezzio was going to find a way. No doubt about it.

"Let's go," Capezzio said.

He was ready for his close-up, which made it a whole lot easier for me. This is the guy who brazenly knocked on Michelle Pfeiffer's trailer door asking for an autograph. Armed with cameras, we moved in like hunters. Wasting no time to charm his prey, Capezzio approached with a huge smile and a polite request for a photograph. His luck was usually right on.

"Sure, sure," Stone replied, smiling, herself. "Let's see how the boys back at the precinct like this one!"

She snatched Capezzio's hat from his head, placing it on her own crown, then she pulled him close to her, practically cheek-to-cheek, as the beaming cop relished every second.

I snapped the lucky bastard's picture. Unknown to us, there were paparazzi somewhere around who actually took the ensuing photograph for an entertainment tabloid. The picture Officer Capezzio would be extremely proud of ran in one of the weekly editions. And there it was for me, another out-of-the-ordinary photo that I was not a part of. As with Clapton and the mock jam session, or Pacino and Scent of a Woman, or even with a better picture with De Niro, I was nowhere near the level of Capezzio.

Here was a cop, in a national magazine with the most famous

actress in the world wearing his policeman's cap, and there I was, this close, but out of the lens's sight. Still, my photo with Ms. Stone is a very good one, and being that close to the actress earned me another wonderful, bewitching moment.

***

In Brooklyn one afternoon, I was certain that I would get a photo with action star Steven Seagal. But, on that day, the actor never emerged from his camper. Rumor circulated that he was occupied with a young woman who was eager for the actor's attention. There was an endless supply of young women hoping to meet celebrities and, like James Woods on The Hard Way set, Seagal was only too happy to oblige.

***

Like a love affair that ends with uncertainty, so, too, was my pending departure.

My last photo in the Movie TV Unit would come by way of a country music video.

Officer Taylor and I were assigned in Greenwich Village on a Lorrie Morgan music shoot that was taking place at a romantic outdoor café. I did not follow the country music genre, so I had no idea how big a celebrity Lorrie Morgan was. Another failed photo opportunity.

What was certain was Morgan's cast mate's superstardom. In the video, Kris Kristofferson was Lorrie Morgan's love interest. Officer Taylor and I were indulging in a cup of coffee; it was the same watered-down blend in the same Styrofoam cups that are commonplace on many of the film shoots.

Taylor was hesitant about asking the star for a photo because, as he told me, "The singer's political leanings are extremely too liberal."

I didn't know much about that.

"What the hell?" I exclaimed.

All I knew was that Kristofferson was the cool rocker guy in A Star is Born. It turned out that the singer was very pleasant when we asked him for a picture. In fact, as we were in the process, a priest happened by and asked if he, too, could get a photo.

Kris Kristofferson replied, "Certainly." Three quick photos, and that was it.

Suddenly, it didn't seem so long ago that I acquired my dream detail.

***

I spent my remaining days on the set of A Bronx Tale. At least I didn't have to trudge into Manhattan any longer. Those last days brought no surprises, as the set was just a flow of easygoing tours. De Niro was always on set.

One more, I thought. I had been too excited the last time, practically elbowing the actor. Ah, too late.

The weather was predictably cool as fall was approaching, and, strangely, I felt a similar climate change coinciding with a new move within the department. Three years ago, the allure of movies pulled me towards the gathering flock. It was a dream that failed to hold my complete attention.

"That's a Wrap"

On November 3, 1992, with no great fanfare, and with no background music, I was finally out. I can't even remember the name of the sergeant who showed up on the set and told me to call the office.

As of November 5th, I was assigned to the 111 Precinct in Bayside, Queens. I'd waited a long time for this moment, almost a year. I had bitched and moaned about my various displeasures about the Movie Unit constantly. Now it was too late for regrets.

The Movie Unit was something that had been awarded to me like a prize. It was not, by any means, an easily attainable detail. I needed phone calls to get in, but I also needed phone calls to get out and land on my feet somewhere that would be comfortable for me.

It was natural to reflect on my three years in the unit, the business of movie making throughout the city, the friends I had made, the brief meetings with celebrities, and the good memories. Alas, we always remain fond of the good.

I remained for two more meaningless days in the bluster of fall. I tried to rationalize about the moments I really disliked – the bone-chilling nights, the extreme boredom, the impossible traffic conditions, the terrible feeling of being regarded as hired security rather than as a real police officer. The crazy schedules with hours changing from day to day, and forced overtime putting in double shifts. Finally, and unfortunately, there was the movie industry itself.

No group is negative as a whole, but the industry is what it is, filled with subservient underlings yearning to be somebody. Publicists and production people – even caterers and bodyguards – thought they held some kind of celebrity status. However, and thankfully, that did not describe the police officers of the Movie Unit.

I did feel for those ambiguous ones, the underlings who treaded lightly, all hoping to climb that ladder to their dream. I admired their tenacity.

I had traveled the Yellow Brick Road of dreams. I had sidestepped the names of legends that were engraved on bronze stars along the sidewalks of Hollywood Boulevard. I had witnessed pop culture up front, and I was privy to the greatest show on earth. The average Joe will always wonder what it would be like to be so close to a celebrity that you could touch him or her, even if it meant being brushed off.

Celebrity has been, and always will be, our country's obsession. Hell, we elect presidents for their celebrity rather than for their policies. Pick up any newspaper or view any news show and celebrity is in your face, often taking precedence over the real news of the day.

What is it like to be waited on hand and foot? What is it like to have the dream automobile, the cottage on the beach, or the villa in Tuscany? What is it like to have no worries about taking time off from work because of illness? What is it like to live an ageless lifestyle and be noticed everywhere?

Who doesn't wonder about such privileges? Stargazers fanatically want to identify with celebrity.

"If Al could be happy as a single man, well, then, so could I!"

"If Swayze could admirably stay married all those years, well, then, I could, too."

"If those people could marry rich, I could, too."

"If Liz could marry a thousand times…"

"To be handsome, to be beautiful…"

"To push the boundaries of the law…"

I ask myself many times about a practice of which I, also, have been guilty.

Why not admire more positive role models, such as folks who love and adore their families positively and unconditionally? Why not admire the honest, everyday man—a truly benevolent soul, a true patriot—who acts without craving accolades? How about the Pope? How crazy is all this?

Is it because we are attracted to the major flaws in other people and do not want to recognize our own? Or are we bewitched by the highs—the idea that celebrities are so in love and so happy?

Is it more interesting to read gossip and scandal? Is it that the wholesome story is boring? Certainly, people indulge in morbid curiosity while rubbernecking at a crawl to watch the big car crash rather than slowing down to watch the guy changing a flat tire.

Being neither psychologist nor priest, I cannot assess the depths of anyone's psyche or unfulfilled dreams. I can only relate the details of my issues, while still trying to shake off the seduction of an industry that preys upon naïveté, much like the endless infomercials that lure the believing caller into purchasing something that has no value.

I began to watch less and less celebrity news and barely read the rag magazines in which the scribbles are forever similar and recycled for each published story.

"Sources close to the star...."

"An insider to the couple says...."

"A friend of the entourage says they are so in love."

"...saw them quarreling."

And so it goes, on and unbelievably on. But I'm sure if I were still in the Movie Unit and involved with celebrity-obsessed folks, I would be pulled toward that wonderment again.

What would it have been like if I remained in the unit for many years? I would have loved to meet more celebrities, especially the biggies like Jack and Meryl. With the influx of a new generation of stars filling the streets of New York, with their followers numbering in the thousands, and with the advent of cell phone cameras, it would certainly have been interesting, especially for the paparazzi.

Capezzio, who eventually had to retire, would have loved it, too. He was the epitome of a fan, possessing great temerity and a uniform that helped fulfill his obsessions. I think about all the times he directed traffic or procured an exaggerated and unneeded escort duty hoping to be appreciated, hoping to find an "in" to a celebrity.

Eventually, the real stinger became a personal one when I failed to take the Police Department's sergeant's test seriously. That dream died on a one-hundred-question test. The unflagging truth was that I did not study with any diligence. My inability to attain the stripes of sergeant nagged at me for quite some time. Actually, I could say I ran with that failure for the rest of my career.

Funny, if those questions had been about the entertainment world, I would have scored a 100%.

I was certainly not one to achieve a thousand arrests, so, sitting back as a supervisor would have been ideal. When I left the unit, I immediately wondered if I had taken a step backwards to patrol, where cops are the low rung on the ladder. It was an irony I would not soon forget. If I had passed the sergeant's test, would I have always harbored the fantasy of returning to the Movie Unit as a boss, free to roam from set to set?

Reality hit me on my first day back in patrol at the 111 Precinct when the administrative lieutenant informed me during orientation that my career would be like starting over. Though technically speaking, I had seniority in the precinct, I was still new and would have to work the graveyard shift with many of the rookies. I was totally bummed.

I remembered thinking about my first days in the Movie Unit when I was assigned to the Richard Crenna movie in Brooklyn. A light mist had begun to fall under the bright movie lamps, and it appeared to glow like an ethereal beacon in the sky.

Now, there were no bright lights, no Radio City and plush carpets, no wrap parties, no Pacino sightings, and no streets where some celebrity might happen by. There was only the darkness of the midnight shift and the blinding sun shining through my windshield as I would endure the early morning trek home. Try as I might, it wasn't going to be easy dashing the stars from my eyes.

The choice I made was as clear as the decision I had made years earlier when I decided not to pursue acting. I still read newspapers and, when I come to a paparazzi shot of a celebrity, especially one of the New York actors, I wonder, what if I were there?

If I'm driving and I see a camper on the move, I wonder, is it a traveling family, or is the trailer bound for a movie set?

My obsession that began long ago, the aggrandizing of celebrity royalty, has lessened ten-fold from those days, but may never be gone completely. It's just easier now to remove myself from the red carpet syndrome, especially with its crop of disillusioned new celebrities and reality stars.

The Movie Unit still exists today, and I am certain that every cop who passes through it is seduced by the same excitement I felt on my short journey. Hopefully, they won't feel the same disappointment, as if the lights had dimmed on Broadway. Every once in a while, I catch the ending credits of a movie and see, way down at the bottom, the very small note of appreciation: "Thank You to the NYPD Movie and TV Unit."

A writing instructor once asked me, "If your house, God forbid, were on fire, what pictures would you save first, your family photos or your celebrity pictures?"

I laughed. "Hey, I worked hard for those pictures."

Epilogue

The enigma for a person with obsessive behavior is that there does not seem to be a happy medium. This means that one is locked in a constant state of ambivalence about life. Is it black or white? Is it good or bad? Social situations, personal relationships, and professional responsibilities must be as close to satisfactory as humanly possible. It is truly hard on the soul.

It was not enough for me to appreciate my good fortune in landing a dream detail in the NYPD. It was necessary to live up to the image I had fantasized about. I wanted to fit in, like a hand in a well-worn glove.

What a pretentious idea. It was presumptuous of me to believe that everything to my liking would come to pass. Of course, that could never really happen; therefore, my reality always led to failure.

Now, I don't want to sound preachy, because much of the celebrity propaganda did win me over for a long time. However, hero worship, though part of the human condition, should not give shape to our own aspirations, nor should the notion of celebrity become the embodiment of our ideals.

Years after my departure from the film unit, I still sigh at the thought of what should have been. There are certain movies I have yet to see more than once because of such feelings of photographic failure. Scent of a Woman leads the pack of my doubts.

I listened with great interest to what Italian-American writer, Gay Talese, articulated during a lecture he gave at Queens College. His message to the listeners in the auditorium was sincere and not condescending. He was hopeful that more Italian-Americans would take an interest in the arts, especially in the art of writing. He wished that many would, at least, read more and collect more books to shelve in their homes.

At the end of the lecture, I asked Mr. Talese to sign the program and to please write this phrase: "Keep writing." I thought that might encourage me to write more.

I read that Mr. Talese had never been formally introduced to Frank Sinatra when he wrote his famous piece, "Sinatra Has a Cold." However, I got the impression that he greatly admired the singer. And that is how I felt. After my experience in the Movie Unit, I was still able to admire Sinatra from afar. In my mind's eye, I could always see the Rat Pack in their iconic stage, and I could honor their unique definition of cool. I could also still admire the work of some of the celebrities I had seen up close, even though I did not enter their inner circle.

After I left the Movie Unit, I finally married. It was a wonderful affair with well over two hundred people. Christine could not have looked more beautiful. After many salutations, I finally found a free moment and was about to dive into my pasta. Just as I sat down to eat, my cousin and his wife came over and asked for a picture of Christine and me.

Instead of being flattered, I felt a twinge of irritation because I had taken a million pictures that day and just wanted to eat. However, as I stood, I instantly felt remorse at how I reacted, and I hoped my cousin didn't notice.

When I sat back down, I thought about the discomfort a celebrity must go through always being asked to take pictures. There again is a paradox, because, truth be told, a celebrity knows that attention comes with the territory. No matter how many of them preach that it's the theater they love, the reality is that they expect to become movie stars, and so flees their anonymity.

They certainly cannot be happy much of the time, though I doubt they would feel the guilt that I did at my wedding. Only in the movies, my friends.